One simple practice that changes everything.

The physics of letting go—
and wanting what's meant for you

Danielle LaPorte

Also available as an audiobook and e-book.

Bless & Release:
The physics of letting go...
and wanting what's meant for you

Danielle LaPorte

Also available as an audiobook, and a workshop template for facilitators

Paperback ISBN 978-1-7346794-3-4
Audiobook ISBN 978-1-7346794-5-8
eBook ISBN 978-1-7346794-4-1

Printed and distributed by Ingram on acid-free paper.

Published by Danielle LaPorte, Inc
125A-1030 Denman Street, Vancouver BC, V6G2M6 Canada

DanielleLaPorte.com

 @daniellelaporte | #blessandrelease

Book Team
Content + Production: *David Di Pardo, Mellissa Last, Lea McGing, Jenn Orajay, Sue Ruhe, Dana Tartal* • Cover Design: *Shyanne Batchelor* • Interior Design: *Shyanne Batchelor, Olga Pomazanova* • Copy Edit: *Arin Murphy-Hiscock, Kathryn Willms* • Proofreader: *Sarah Newton-John*

MEDIA + SPEAKING: please contact media@daniellelaporte.com
SALES: for discounts and bulk purchases, please contact sales@daniellelaporte.com
ALL INQUIRIES: support@daniellelaporte.com
For access to the Bless & Release Bonuses: daniellelaporte.com/blessbonus

A disclaimer note on healing and professional support: This content is for spiritual direction and emotional transformation—it's not medical advice, therapy, or a substitute for professional mental health support. Please honour your individual needs.

Created purely with *authentic* intelligence. Not one sentence in this book is written by artificial intelligence. This is an original expression of human creativity—which includes a longstanding adoration of em dashes.

Praise

"Danielle LaPorte is **a bright light...** She keeps it spiritual, she keeps it real."
—**Marianne Williamson**, *NY Times bestselling author of* A Return to Love

"**A beacon of compassion**, Danielle is an extraordinary human. Honest, accessible and authentic to the core."
—**Rich Roll**, *host of* Rich Roll Podcast, *vegan activist, and athlete*

"Danielle is a **force field of energy, wonder, humor, and love.**"
—**V (formerly Eve Ensler)**, *author of* The Vagina Monologues

"Danielle's voice is **medicine for self-help fatigue and ambition overdrive.**"
—**Dr. Mark Hyman**, *10-time* New York Times *bestselling author*

"She's the **Real Deal!**"
—**Rev. Michael Beckwith**, *founder of Agape International Spiritual Center*

"Danielle is the Stevie Nicks of spiritual teachers."
—**John Kim**, *aka The Angry Therapist, author of* Single on Purpose: Redefine Everything. Find Yourself First.

"...a woman who's made a tremendous impact on my life with her **brave and badass approach to living a heart centered life.**"
—**LeAnn Rimes**, *singer/songwriter, host of the* Wholly Human Podcast

"Danielle is the living **embodiment of heart centered leadership.**"
—**John Wineland**, *founder of The New Men's Work Project, author of* From the Core

TABLE OF CONTENTS

Hello, friend.

It's an honour to hear what people want to let go of.

I've asked thousands.

Responses are always immediate and emphatic. We know where it hurts, even if we don't know why, or what to do about it. We *want* to talk about it—we need to—because we don't talk about it enough.

What do you want to let go of? is a hot question because letting go leads to mental lucidity and love. And in a world of fakery and f*ckery, we need more of that kind of common sense.

What do you want to manifest? is an equally powerful question. Because, as Proverbs teaches, without vision we perish. Manifesting comes with its own complications. Some of us run ragged trying to manifest our bucket lists. Some of us think we need to prove that we're worthy of what we want. Some of us have cracked the code of surrendering with just the right amount of striving.

Both letting go and manifesting require us to tap into our creative agency and trust. That's what I'm most interested in: using our freewill to choose what's good for us and walk away from the rest—with grace.

Say it with me now, "I choose what's good for me." Repeat as needed.

I love questions that get asked for the right reasons. I love pattern recognition and emotional intimacy. And I love The Light. So it makes sense that I've spent so much of my life trying to figure out why people really want what they want.

I ran a future studies think tank in Washington, D.C., where we built predictive scenarios exploring how global trends might converge—or collide. That was trippy. I've spent 15 years studying desire—and therefore aversion—through the lenses of Buddhism and desire, shadow work and desire, and pop psychology and desire. It's been a lot of desire.

And you *know* that I took and taught all the workshops: Inner Child visualization, data visualization, visionary art, the art of manifestation.

Exploring and understanding the contradictions within people—including myself—has taught me what keeps us stuck and what uncorks Joy. And by contradictions, I mean our humanness in all its glimmering light and shadows, assorted pasts, and courageous ambitions.

It's clear: The people who let go more easily are more joyful, *and* they create more deliberately. It's not that they have fewer challenges; it's that those challenges just don't derail them for long. They reframe problems as problems show up. They don't avoid their pain, but they don't guard against it either.

The letting-go'rs have a very different relationship to suffering than the hanger-on'rs.

Lots of people have manifested their versions of success. But the ones who know how to hold discomfort while circulating optimism are the ones who really *enjoy and share* their success. They know how to stay centered.

I've paid attention to how letting go plays out with a lot of people, especially in the spiritual wellness space. I've sat with gurus who were great at business because they held firm to a vision. I've hung out with biohackers who couldn't let go of their unhealthy mindsets. I've worked with meditation teachers who clung to their desire for enlightenment. And I've learned from metaphysical practitioners who hold the suffering of humanity but have let go of society.

Each of them taught me about letting go and magnetism.

My personal experience of letting go has been... humbling. And awesome.

I let go of a lifestyle that I had overworked to build—a big house, big closet, big striving. I gave away truckloads of things, sold my car, consigned my dresses, and hit pause on public speaking. "Downsized" would be an understatement.

Before that, every few years, like a bird with a funky migration pattern, I'd imagine flying away from it all. I'd consider shaving my head, deleting my Instagram profile, and finding a monastery that would accommodate me and all my supplements—and ideally my friends when they needed a getaway. I could be reclusive and meditate all day but still host dinner parties! I would be so enlightened that I wouldn't care about the algorithm or email.

You can see the contradictions.

This was a spiritually romantic kind of torture: the belief that radical letting go of my worldly desires would finally bring me peace—and good karma. In actuality, I was using both my spiritual *and* entrepreneurial identities to guilt-trip myself. I told myself that I wasn't tolerant enough, successful enough, or 5D enough. I came to the conclusion that it was best to be… D. Myself.

It took a lot of self-compassion—which is the ultimate self-help.

As part of the process, I connected with the fear driving the hustle that never let me rest. And then—deep breath—I renounced my relationship with renunciation. Which is to say, I stopped using spiritual perfectionism to punish myself.

I learned to welcome in emotional pain and shame—and both face it and embrace it. And I healed (and am still healing) the habit of compulsively criticizing myself for having "unspiritual" feelings and very human needs.

My healing happened over a decade. (It won't take you as long because I'm going to help you flatten your learning curve.)

**One focused breath at a time,
I became a Super Blesser.**

How did I resolve long-standing, deeply ingrained, harmful behavioural patterns in order to create a life I love?

I stopped criticizing myself for having long-standing, deeply ingrained, harmful behavioural patterns.

Instead of trying to eliminate my fears and desires, I *actively* (key word here) started applying compassion to them. I stopped trying to make my fears and desires go away.

I prioritized my nervous system. I formed a habit of leading with curiosity instead of critique. Multiple times a day, I applied light and breath to both my anxieties and my life visions. I learned to stay centered.

One simple practice held me: The Centering Practice.
And I'm going to teach you how to use it every day to change your life.

This is a heart centered way to live. I've seen it lead to incredible shifts in family and romantic relationships. It's helped thousands of my readers and listeners create peace where there was pain, and grace where there was struggle.

It helped me let go of two marriages and the shame of letting go of two marriages. It helped me dissolve heaps of guilt and unhealthy patterning around my needs, wants, weaknesses, and strengths. And ultimately, it led me create a life where I manifest from Joy—I'm not held back by the fear of not getting what I want.

I did not let go of limiting thoughtforms by endlessly talking about my limiting thoughtforms. I did not shift old patterns by rehashing unmet needs. I did not arrive at Joy by trying to prove to God and the internet that I was doing good things and was therefore worthy of Joy.

Letting go meant I had to stop assigning my experiences and feelings (and other people) to the categories of "positive" or "negative." I learned to stay open and neutralize my extreme reactions. In the process, I became less triggerable (I think this is the best result of becoming more heart centered). I had to stop using labels, like "introvert, Gemini-Virgo, spiritual baller," as an excuse to be an outsider judging everyone else's life decisions and font choices.

But what I should be saying about all of this "letting go" is that I started to *let things in*. I started *bringing my thoughts and feelings into the center of my heart, instead of pushing them away or trying to make them behave.*

I started doing the energy work that I'd previously outsourced to healers and other such authorities.

Now I'm here to help you do the same.

Trust in divine timing

For decades—even before the turn of the millennium—big thinkers have been saying that we're living in "unprecedented times." Every year, we seem to up the ante: "No, *this* is unprecedented."

We've become accustomed to pushing away pain and chasing desire, to treating propaganda like actual wisdom. The result is predictable: anxiety and exhaustion.

I'm watching people turn to artificial intelligence for spiritual direction. *Please.*

I'm seeing friends lose family to politics and unravelling in the process. Many of us are wondering how to reconcile "manifestation techniques" with the state of the world. Healers who give "You can have it all" sermons seem to set us up for failure. And how can we "raise our vibration" given the depth of grief that needs to be honoured?

We're arguing over what's sacred. We're overwhelmed.

We need to get centered.

You don't need to know if it's Kali Yuga or the Age of Aquarius.
Your nervous system knows what time it is.
It's time to heal.

We need a new relationship with our emotions, ambitions, and all things manifestation. Because, clearly, the current one is not working. A lot of us are in a lot of pain, and we need to do something radical about it.

Here's a radical idea: Instead of repressing, rejecting, or ignoring our suffering, we bring it even closer. Within. Gently. Continuously. *As if we were blessing it.*

As if we were alchemists and energy workers.

Because we are.

I'm so glad you're here.

With Love,

Danielle

XO

What we push away
pushes back—
and gets stronger.

What we embrace
transforms—
and strengthens us.

Chapter 1

Principles of Bless & Release

1. **Want what's meant for you.** Be inspired from within, not pulled out by grandiose goals. Clear the path so what's truly yours can come to you.

2. **What we push away pushes back—and grows stronger. What we embrace transforms—and strengthens us.**

3. **Resilience comes from integrating our emotions, not rejecting them.** We create inner balance with curiosity and compassion for our feelings—especially the "not so positive" feelings.

4. **The heart—the seat of the Soul—is the command center.** Change only happens through the heart. Healing and manifesting are energy work, not purely a mental exercise.

5. **The Soul uses the mind as a tool for manifesting.** It's the instrument that creates structures and realities. We're manifesting all the time, consciously and unconsciously.

6. **Meaningful manifestation is the result of coherence.** It's a by-product of being heart centered. Harnessing life energy to *be* what you want, not only to get what you want, is a very powerful way to live.

7. **Behind every desire there's an aversion.** Don't run away from the negatives. Run towards the positives. Focus on what you do want.

8. **Energy follows thought.** So, what's the energy of your thoughts? Think higher, desire higher.

9. **We are not our feelings, but we do create most of our feelings.** Our emotions are "mind babies" that we need to lovingly parent.

10. **Nothing changes until we accept it.** When we stop trying to "fix" our experience, something shifts. Everything we create—feelings, relationship dynamics, illnesses—circles back for attention until it gets Love and Acceptance.

11. **We can do intense work gently.** In fact, the gentle approach creates the most powerful change.

12. **Clinging to impermanent things creates suffering. Letting go creates Joy.**

13. **Focus on what you want, but release attachment to the outcome.** Whatever the result, you will become a more conscious creator.

14. **Reframe obstacles as portals to better possibilities.**

15. **True letting go happens when there are no expectations of what will result from it.** And letting go helps you realize that more is already on its way.

16. **Balancing the nervous system has to be a top priority.** Heart-brain-body coherence sets the best conditions for fulfilling manifestation.

17. **You are not the wound. You are the healer.**

18. **We heal the world by healing ourselves**, which is done by loving the world.

19. **How we perceive ourselves influences what we attract.** We incarnate to remember our Divine Identity.

20. **Conscious creation is entirely dependent on Faith.** Faith is like the railroad track that our visions travel on.

21. **Conscious creation is interdependent.** We can take radical responsibility while collaborating with the collective, trusting our Soul to orchestrate it all.

Chapter 2

Bring it in

There are things we want, and things we want to let go of.

Things we hope will go away, and things we wish had never happened.

We all have so much to heal and to make happen at the same time: shedding old ways, dissolving obstacles, dreaming new dreams, holding space, making space, learning how to take up more space... or less space, depending on the space you're in.

Most of us live between the past that we long for, the past we're trying to get over, and the future we're trying to manifest.

This might seem like an obvious moment to talk about being present and the power of the now—to remind you that everything is happening all at once, everywhere, across multiple dimensions. That, cosmically speaking, the past never really happened, and the future timeline is yours to choose.

All of this may be true. But I've never found those universal laws that comforting when I'm in pain or trying to get a project off the ground. In those moments, most of the time, what's most practical—and powerful—is to stay in my body and connect with my heart.

There's a reason getting centered is at the root of spiritual practices throughout time.

Spiritual practice is really just the process of learning to create with more intention. It's about *conscious* creation rather than unconscious creation—which tends to make a big mess of things.

We may think that we're consciously creating with our vision boards and quarterly objectives. This can be true, but manifesting culture can also make us frantic.

There are unpredictable nervous systems, emotional triggers, and unmet needs to take into consideration. Not to mention decision-making habits, lineage and culture, and our karma.

Nothing can shift until there's Acceptance—not the pain we carry, not the future we're waiting on. I'm not talking here about the conditional acceptance granted when standards are met, i.e., "I am sufficiently pleased, therefore I accept this." The virtue of Acceptance is actually radical.

Acceptance is meeting whatever shows up in your life as if you ordered it. Out of all the virtues, Acceptance may be the most spiritually badass. It's the degree of consciousness that helps you cut through confusion quickly and see the next best move.

Letting go and manifesting are both about transformation.

In both processes, we're healing the feelings that have held us back. We're upleveling our identity to magnetize a reality that matches how we see ourselves. And we're changing how we perceive the past, the present, and the future so that what's truly meant for us can take form. We're transforming perception into reality.

Both letting go and manifestation are forms of conscious creation.

Releasing and magnetizing are ways we go about shifting from the current state to a higher state.

Real transformation only happens in the heart space, the center of our beingness and body. **The heart is the most powerful vortex of change.** Our capacity for focused positive intention—blessing—comes from the heart. Every religion and all mysticism eventually arrive at the same insight: after all the physical sacrifice and mind training, the portal to liberation is through the heart.

Love alchemizes everything it touches.

Love is practical

Love is the mother of all virtues. She births all the other virtues: Compassion, Forgiveness, Joy, Acceptance, Generosity. Love is our Original Essence—the substance of all things made manifest. It's heaven meeting Earth, where the holy meets the human. Beingness embodied. We are made by Love, because of Love, as Love.

To love something—a person, a neighbourhood, an idea—is to bless it.

Very *practically* speaking, though, what is the application of Love? For example, in the context of managing pain or getting projects off the ground? Or emotional intimacy and relationships? What's Divine Love got to do with prosperity and a healthy body?

Being loving is how we consciously create our lives. It's the formula for letting go *and* for making good things happen. Letting go is not about cutting something out of your life. And manifesting is not about pushing something to happen, because Love is neither of these things.

Stay with me.

I know there are things you want to let go of; we all carry longings in our hearts.

Some of those longings get our intentional focus—a very useful mental skill. Others receive our attention without intention, becoming habitual, default patterns: the thoughts we think all the time without being aware we're thinking them. There's also negative focus, which is just a drag on our energy.

And then there's focused positive intention. When you give focused positive attention to whatever's in front of you, you're embodying Love.

This is a very powerful trifecta: mental stamina meeting benevolence and will.

When you willingly give your focus to something, you stream the light of your consciousness on it. Light given becomes Love. And to give your focused positive intention to anything is to bless it.

> *Your attention is an intentional focused gaze, placing your mindful awareness on a given experience without being swept away by ruminating thoughts.*
> —V.S.

You can give your focused positive intention to your feelings, visions, resistance, and brilliance.

You can give your focused positive intention to people you love, and to those who aren't as easy to love. To broken bones and test results, to the rivers and the forests. To new birthdays and launches. To trauma and the memories that play on repeat. To your longing for love and success in all forms.

When you give your focused positive intention to something, you center it in your heart and bless it. You pour Compassion on anxiety, and saturate the inner vision board with Faith.

Your Love changes whatever it's focused on. For the better. Always.

Focused positive intention is life-changing.

Blessing your pain raises its frequency to something *less painful.*

Then it goes back into your energy field lighter, and more *manageable.*

Blessing what you have generates gratitude, which magnetizes more to be grateful for.

Blessing your visions makes what you're visualizing more magnetic.

Then you release that desire into the energy field to be made manifest.

Letting go of what you *don't* want and manifesting what you *do* want *are the same power move.*

Bless & Release is the new letting go

I'm reading your mind right now. I know that there's something you want to release, dissolve, and be free of. Ya?

And... you're probably tired of holding on and holding it together. Ya?

I also know that you are not your past, your pain, or your patterns of rejection or regret.

> **You are not the wound.**
> *You are the healer.*

Healing happens when we let go of thoughtforms, untruths, excesses, and all those things that stopped working a long time ago. Not to mention the things that never really worked for us.

Letting go is about *circulating energy.*

Manifesting is about *circulating energy.*

Which makes you an energy worker. Maybe even a Super Blesser.

The first lesson in this masterclass in letting go is a paradox: we can't *actually* let anything go.

This isn't philosophy—it's physics, one of the natural laws that we already live by.

> **Energy can't be destroyed;**
> **it can only be transformed.**

Healing isn't about building walls or cutting cords because what we banish always comes back, wanting to belong. Like that old friend who just wants some validation. Our pain and heartbreak are meant to be processed into power—and circulated back into Love.

Letting go—for real—is about *integration*. Alchemy, not annihilation.

All of our freedom and power lie in this truth.

. . .

You are magnetic

Your thoughts function like little magnets in your energy field. And I'm not speaking here only metaphorically or metaphysically. The brain is an electromagnetic organ, constantly receiving and transmitting energy.

"Like attracts like" isn't just spiritual wisdom—it's quantum field theory, which describes how conscious observation influences what's being observed.

When you observe your difficult feelings—or people you find difficult—with curiosity and compassion, you're not just being "nice." You're applying fundamental physics to bring order to disorder, because thoughtforms of a similar nature attract more of the same and vitalize more easily and faster. Once we really understand the implications of this, we get *very* intentional about our choice of thoughts.

"Negative" thoughts allow more negative thoughts to creep in from the subconscious—misery loves company—until you end up with a cluster of negative thoughts.

On the other hand, when we have a "positive" thought, it will start to generate more positive thoughts—and more reasons to support our positive thinking.

The more you think certain thoughts, the more defined those neural pathways become. This is neuroplasticity, the ability of the brain to change its neural pathways. It means your repeated thought patterns are physically rewiring your brain's structure! And this will influence your internal chemistry, which informs your moods and choices.

Focused positive intention—the act of blessing or lovin' something—creates harmony in chaotic energy systems.

In other words, Compassion creates order.

Blessing your emotional triggers doesn't just soothe you; it transforms your behavioural patterns, opening new ways of being *and relating.* When you work at the quantum level like this, you're using energy to organize your experience. In that sense, blessing your struggles, hopes, and desires isn't a hypnotic affirmation. It's a way of accessing a deeper field of intelligence—the universal mind.

Heart work can be hard work. Some days we have to work through ugly things. Scary and heavy things. But not only can it be done gently, it has to be done gently. There's no such thing as a forceful blessing. Emphatic, yes. Pushy? No.

Of course, we want to push away pain. And of course, we want to pull on our desires. This is so human and understandable, it's kind of charming. Rejection and striving come naturally to us.

But it doesn't really work, does it? Because that push and pull goes against the inseparable laws of both esoterica and science. Life does not come into form through force. It's all about magnetism and attraction. Focus and flow. Focused positive intention.

How we relate

We have to be *in relationship* with our fears, not in opposition to them.

Most fear is based on past experiences that we then project onto our future. It's a draining inner battle, making and then trying to fight what we created (our fear). It's the insanity of aggressively trying to let something go. It's the cognitive dissonance of gripping what we desperately want to put down. It's one of the least fruitful human strategies ever.

Relax your grip; you deserve relief. After all, we're all Divinity athletes in the game of life, and it's really the Soul that's calling the shots. All of our experiences are being delivered by our Higher Self. And what our fear is really masking is the discomfort of being uncertain about our future—and the pain of holding on to past hurts.

So instead of resenting the f*ck out of our challenges, let's get more creative. Resentment, by the way, is a major abundance blocker. The less resentment we haul around, the more we magnetize pleasure. Less ego, more eagerness to learn.

Less resistance, more leaning in.

How do we let go of our fear of letting go? We bring it into the heart center. Breathe a bit. Pour some light on it. Let it relax.

How do we actualize our plans for abundance, in all its forms? Same move. Bring it into the heart center. Let it relax.

We tend to forget how healing relaxation is. The state of relaxation—of trust—is magnetic.

Indestructible you

I can't say that quantum field theory has ever crossed my mind when I'm arguing with someone or feeling misunderstood. Nope. When someone slides into my DMs all unhinged with opinions about my opinions, I don't stop and think, "Energy can't be destroyed; it can only be transformed." Nope, I don't.

I can be spicy and intolerant. My memory for who said what (and what they were wearing when they said it) is not always in everyone's favour. My customer service standards are ridiculously high. And for someone who's a natural love bug, I can be really aloof—and worse, not really care about being aloof.

But even in the stressy times, I know that I want to love as much as I want to be loved. Resonance is my favourite. Always.

I want to bless & release everyone's bad behaviour and weirdo ways, including my own, so that we can get back to loving. So I breathe. I bring the experience—the frustration or the brilliant vision of my desire—into the center of my heart. And I pour light on it. I let it relax. Then I relax. Sometimes I cry. Mostly I feel... *possible.* I am the queen of my own manifestation mandala. I am centered.

We all deeply long for harmony. It's an inbuilt psychological need. Studies show that if we do not feel in sync with another person, it affects our cognition and memory. Lack of harmony is literally confusing because it's not our divinely natural state.

Our favourite physics principle applies to psychology too. The fundamental therapeutic framework is, you guessed it, *energy can't be destroyed; it can only be transformed.* Meaning: the shit happened. Let's compost it into some Wisdom flowers.

In other words, the body stores what we do not express. When we suppress our emotions, they don't vanish. Unexpressed anger can shapeshift into resentment or depression.

Circulating energy is how nature thrives, and also how both the anatomical and the spiritual heart function. Mental health abides by the laws of physics.

The healing framework is only complete when we include the Soul, the heart—*the source of all conscious creation.*

Ancient traditions teach that the Soul's essence is eternal—without beginning and without end, and always evolving. This is the *best* news ever. It confirms that...

You cannot be destroyed; you can only be transformed.

The Centering Practice: FYIs

PREPARE

- **The Centering Practice is for focused positive intention—blessing.** You're directing the light of your consciousness where you want it to go. This is an act of Love.
- This practice can be done in a few minutes or less, or as a long-form meditation. It can be done in stillness or in motion, and at any time of day, though mornings are ideal, and before sleep is excellent. It's all helpful.
- It's best to practice when you're feeling balanced. If you're in the middle of an emotional surge, give yourself time to get calm.
- **SET YOUR INTENTION.** Do you want to **heal** something? Or **manifest** something?
    - » **If you're healing a challenge**: Focus on blessing just one aspect of the situation at a time—you don't have to work with it all at once. We're moving stagnancies from the Lower Mind into the heart space to be healed.
    - » **If you're manifesting a vision**: Bring specific success scenes into your heart. Focus on one at a time. Make them vivid and alive.
- **How to "bring something into the heart"**: Focus on a word or phrase, a snapshot of a moment, or a symbol, face, place, or landscape. You could also hear a word or a soundscape.
- **If you don't see mental images:** Try simply thinking "Light" or "Healing," and trust your brain's processing to do the rest. You may also want to verbally walk through the practice or create sensory anchors, such as focusing on the warmth in your chest, the rhythm of your breath, or the word "Light."
- **Easy does it.** If you feel like you're getting more triggered, not less, then do the practice for shorter periods of time. The medicine is often in the dose.

The Centering Practice

Bring it into your heart. Heal and manifest.

1. **Breathe.** Place your right hand on your heart for a few breaths.
2. **Positive thought.** Bring to mind a beautiful memory, feeling, or virtue. This helps your mind relax.
3. **Gold light.** Imagine warm, golden light filling your heart.
4. **Bring what you're healing or manifesting into your heart.** See the scene, moment, word, symbol, or thought in the center of your heart.
5. **Light spectrum.** Shine rainbow colours on what you're blessing—like light moving through stained glass. Work with colours that feel soft but dynamic and alive. These are healing frequencies.
   Pinks, peach tones, golds, minty greens, sky blues, light purples.
6. **Add in virtues if you like.** You can project or speak higher qualities into your heart center, such as Compassion, Love, Joy, Forgiveness...
7. **Important: Let what you've blessed relax in your heart.** There's no need to fixate on it or analyze it. Now that you've done the energy work, let the expansion happen.

Repeat as you like, in daily moments or as a long-form meditation.

The anatomy of blessings

> *Those who succeed in turning misfortune into blessing, and gloom into hope, have discovered the true art of living—they have become conscious coworkers with the creative forces of Nature.*
> —Master Beinsa Douno

- **A blessing is a *focused positive intention.*** It's how we consciously create our lives: manifesting and letting go, energizing our higher intentions, and healing our emotional discomforts. It's especially effective for working with unfriendly sensations and negative feelings. Blessing is a way of life.
- Blessing is a simple practice: **we center *everything* in our heart, and by acknowledging it and treating it with compassion, *we raise its vibration.*** This is a way of circulating high-frequency energy—which creates health in all systems.
- **Blessing is a cleansing mechanism.** In our day-to-day lives—where we're inundated with messages and images, overly busy, and running from our aversions—we can become irritable, and our thinking can get disorganized. All these incoming energies can create congestion, depleting our energy field. This has a cascade effect on our chakras, organs, and body systems. When we practice our blessing protocols consistently, we're energetically purifying, and *that* leads to Joy and wellbeing!
- **Focused positive intention aligns us with our visionary, higher states of consciousness.** This is not a mental exercise—though it shifts mindsets big time. This is energy work.

- **Blessings aren't just "positive thinking."** Positive thinking is purely mental and can be ego-driven, whereas blessings go beyond the mind. The intention behind blessings is generated in the heart, and the heart cues the mind to align its thoughts, speech, and actions with Love.
- **Blessings are benevolent.** We wish the best outcomes for everyone involved.
- **Blessings are expressions of virtues,** such as Love, Compassion, Generosity, Joy, Loving Kindness... Most blessings can be distilled to Forgiveness or Gratitude.
- **Blessings are the seeds of transformation.** Sending love stimulates hope and change. When we offer blessings, we break vicious cycles.
- **Blessings are given without expectations.** We're offering the unconditional love that we all long for.
- **Blessings boomerang.** The more we bless, the more comes back to us. Blessings are a great wellness plan.
- **Extending blessings dissolves our fears and delusions.** Working with heart intelligence increases consciousness of Oneness—and *that's* what dissipates fear and feelings of helplessness.
- **The more gratitude you feel, the easier it is to be a blesser.** Appreciation is the springboard for Higher Consciousness.
- **Anyone can be a blesser.** It's our True Nature to love in all directions.
- **Blessings dissolve chaos and restore sanity.** They put everything back in Divine Order because blessings are a return to Love.

What Gets Released?

- **Conscious letting go is really about conscious creation.** It's the shift from lower to higher energy states. Low vibe to high vibe. Since energy can't be destroyed, what we feel—whether it's pain or desire—must be transformed into a higher vibration. This is the true definition of progress.
- Release happens when we give something our focused positive intention, bringing it into the heart center. When we put blessing energy on it, it changes state—and begins to flow forward.
- When we bless & release something, we're *sending it back into our energy field*—which is connected to the unified field of life.

The power of The Centering Practice is that it raises the vibration of what's in your energy field.

You become a closer vibrational match to your desires.

You become more loving and lucid.

By bringing what you want to let go of or manifest into your heart center, you bless it with light and good energy. And when you exhale, you release it back into your energy field in a better form, raising your frequency.

This is called healing. And you are the healer.

The Centering Practice is your tool.

Reluctant to bless?

Are you willing to love more today than you did yesterday?

Are you willing to let it go?

We don't have to be fearless. We don't have to have the next steps mapped out to benefit from this practice. We just have to be willing.

What we're really doing here is bringing relaxation to the stress caused by holding on.

If what you want to heal feels too painful to bring into your heart center, love, I get it: some things just feel too jagged to work with right away. If you're not ready to fully let it go, that's okay.

Start small. Do a micro bless. No major incantation or lightshow. Bring just one thought about the gnarly situation into your heart center and take a few breaths. Or say a prayer—prayers are the original blessing. And whenever you're up for more active work with your heart chakra, the timing will be divine. Incremental blessing counts.

It all counts.

How do you see your heart?

Meditate on the Self as being
Vast as the sky.
A body of energy
Extending forever in all directions—
Above, below, all around.
In the embrace of the infinite space,
Awaken to your true form—
Divine creative energy
Revealing Herself as you.
—*The Radiance Sutras*, Sutra 69

The radiant heart through time and history

There's the flaming Sacred Heart of Jesus Christ. Our Lady of Guadalupe, with roses springing from her breast. The Immaculate Heart of Mary, aflame, surrounded by roses, sometimes pierced by swords to symbolize healing sorrow with Divine Love. And Saint Hildegard of Bingen, with her heart of divine fire.

In Hinduism, the heart chakra, also known as the anahata chakra, is depicted as a 12-petaled green lotus flower, sometimes with deities seated within it, a sublime symbol of Love, Compassion, and balance.

We also see radiating hearts in Eastern Orthodox icons. The Kabbalah's Tree of Life corresponds with the heart. In hermetic philosophy, the "emerald heart" or "green lion" are metaphors for the heart chakra and spiritual transformation.

Buddhism's sacred art often shows enlightened masters with glowing hearts: specifically, the Bodhisattvas who are able to reach nirvana but hold off their ascension to stay on Earth and help all suffering beings. One of my favourites, the Medicine Buddha, is usually shown with a glowing blue heart center, holding a healing bowl or lotus.

Buddhists often use the sky as a poetic metaphor for the heart—you are *that* limitless! The clouds passing through are merely thoughts and emotions; you are the environment that holds it all.

Picture your heart center

Having a visual for your heart center helps you connect with it and work with it every day.

Create an image of your heart.

Or a sound. *Ommm.*

Or a gesture. *Hand to heart. Lightly tap your heart chakra three times. Inhale, exhale.*

Or a seed phrase. *Divine Light. Hello love. Here I am.*

I see my heart chakra as a pale blue sky, with every particle lit from within. In the center of that sky is a rainbow spectrum—the colour qualities of light shining through stained glass. Fuchsia pinks, golden yellows, minty greens. Alive.

I experience my heart as the central location of *me*, where small *me* meets my Higher Self. Where heaven touches me on Earth. Here, I'm the pinnacle and all the particles. I'm in Love.

When I bring my problems into the vast landscape of my pale-blue-sky consciousness and rainbow-spectrum heart, my "problems" get really small, really fast. Even if they don't disappear immediately, they become more manageable—simply ideas and emotions floating in my lit-up, loving atmosphere.

Perspective is everything.

Is your heart center a majestic doorway? A kaleidoscopic portal? A chapel full of roses?

A lush forest, smelling fresh and sweet, with running streams and dappled sunlight? A field of sunflowers and singing wind? A mountain peak covered in pristine, shimmering snow?

Is your heart a solar-powered battery pack with big buttons?

An aquamarine ocean being blessed by multiple suns?

An indigo galaxy full of silver stars?

How do you see your heart?

My Bless & Release Journal

Re: Manifesting my visions and healing worry.

I'm walking on the seawall doing my morning Centering Practice. I know that when I do any kind of practice outside, I'm getting extra energy from interacting with the elements.

I always focus first on what I want to manifest. I see my vision in great detail. I project some Joy and Generosity on to it. I pour on the colours. At the same time, I'm giving thanks to the ocean that I'm walking by and the root systems of the trees. I'm really turning up the energy dial. I let the vision go, sending it up into the sky to be taken care of. I remind myself that my heart is as vast as the sky.

Then I switch gears and go to work on any worries that I'm carrying. This particular morning, I'm worried about the burnout and loneliness that might come with achievement. I work with one worry at a time. I'm immediately compassionate with myself. Zero judgment for having worries crossing my mind. I'm happy that I'm aware of them.

I bring each worry into the center of my heart. It gets the same loving attention as my dreams. I let it all relax. I don't think much more about the worry for the rest of the day.

And I assume my visions are being handled.

I do a version of this Centering Practice every single morning. Sometimes walking. Often seated in front of a candle. Once and a while on airplanes. Definitely on solstices and equinoxes. Always with so much Love.

Chapter 3

Blessing works

When you start working with your heart's intelligence, your way of living will shift for the better.

You will have energy for the things that you *actually* want to do. You will stop obsessing—no more mental replays of that conversation from months (or years) ago. You'll stop cataloguing past resentments, and your creativity will surge. You'll trust your ideas again and actually *start the thing you've been wanting to do.*

You will stop bracing for impact. That constant tension of waiting for the other shoe to drop, for something bad to happen? Practicing focused positive intention builds deeper trust.

You will stop managing other people's emotions. This is exciting, isn't it?!

All human interaction requires Loving Kindness and care. 100%. And some people require special handling—for their sake *and* ours.

But...

The constant walking on eggshells—being selective with our words, replaying conversations in our heads, over-apologizing in an attempt to make it better—are no-win behaviour patterns. All this worrying about other people burns through our energy reserves.

We manage other adults' emotions out of fear—fear of loss, rejection, or having the same old argument. This is how the ego tries to protect itself, but it's exhausting, innit?

When you filter your emotions through your heart, you build emotional resilience. Blessing your worries, resentments, fears of abandonment, and beautiful longings makes you more courageous and flexible. You can honour someone else's discomfort while honouring your own.

Your capacity to forgive will amaze you.

I've seen The Centering Practice work its way into people's lives in ways that surprised even them.

While getting ready to rock out at a music festival with her girlfriends, Gina ran into the woman, the mistress, who had broken up her marriage. It was the kind of confrontation moment that could make you freeze.

"When she walked up to me, I said to myself, 'Okay, this is happening.' I took a deep breath into my heart and breathed in the rainbow colours. And I was able to give that out to her as we spoke. I stayed in my heart. So when she asked if I could forgive her, it was true when I said, 'I do forgive you. I also forgive my partner. But most of all, I forgive myself.'"

"And that was the release for me..." Gina said. "The forgiveness of myself. I *never* would have thought that was possible a year ago. But the blessing work *works*." Gina's girlfriend crew was like, "Are you okay?" She was more than okay. She hit the dance floor—best release ritual ever.

That's what happens when we do the daily inner work: dancing instead of drama.

You get back into your body. Your sympathetic nervous system comes into balance. You breathe deeper. You sleep better—your brain stops the 2am highlight reel of problems because you no longer see them as problems.

You will feel grateful without forcing it. Appreciation happens naturally when you're not so busy being pissed off. And more gratitude means more dopamine and other happiness chemicals streaming through your brain and body.

You will have more emotional intimacy in your life. You will pause instead of being offended. You will get closer to the people you really like. When you're not carrying grudges or vibrating with resentment, you have so much more space in your life for real connection.

New things will happen. Miraculous kinds of things involving new people and new opportunities. This is because the heart space is the nucleus of quantum creation, operating beyond our usual frameworks. Every time you apply focused positive intention to something or someone, you tap into that power supply—the generator of miracles.

You'll want for less but know that so much more is possible. Releasing old stories relaxes the hungry ghost inside. When you're a blesser, you conduct more Love, so you're no longer starving for it—and you pour it on every idea, desire, and connection.

Chapter 4

What to Bless & Release

Here are some suggestions for counterintuitive, countercultural, and the most liberating things to bless & release.

Bless & Release: Your fear

> *As long as we are running away from fear, we do not look at it. The moment we stop and look at fear, it begins to dissolve.*
> —J. Krishnamurti, *Life Ahead*

One of the biggest delusions of self-help culture is that rejecting our fears makes us less fearful. Overriding our fears blinds us to what we're actually scared of. And what we can't see can control us.

We can overpower our fears and accomplish amazing things, for sure. We do it all the time. But outer achievements don't guarantee inner growth. Sometimes, bravery is really just bravado covering up insecurities.

We create our own fears. Every single one of our fears and neuroses comes from the unconscious mind. Each one is a "mind baby."

You are the mother/father of your anxiety and phobias. Your job is to parent your fears, not to deny or abandon them, and build a quality relationship with your emotions. Talk to your fears. Engage lovingly. This is how we take deep, inner responsibility for what we ourselves have created. It's also where a lot of us trip up.

Years ago, when I first started connecting with my fears in therapy, I was not very, um, friendly with them. I thought that shadow work was about getting my dark side to behave, and I just needed to put my fear in its place. Also, I was a bit pissed off with my fears. I thought they were costing me opportunities.

We often create toxic relationships with traits we don't like, rejecting them or avoiding them. But discipline and criticism do not heal hurt feelings. Acceptance and self-compassion do.

Fear does not need to be dominated. In fact, trying so hard to control it is an indication that it is actually controlling you.

Blessing it, on the other hand, liberates you, your fear, and your fear of fear.

Bring your fear into your heart and have a conversation with it. "You're afraid of failing? I hear you, I've got you. And the Divine has me. And we're going on this adventure." You could even thank your fear for helping you to become more conscious—because that is its highest purpose.

By doing this, you interrupt a lifelong pattern of rejecting your fear. Instead, you face it and accept it: no fear left behind! And then off you go.

If you carry your fear in your heart, it doesn't hold you back.

Bless & Release: Trying to be confident all the time

Dating surveys show that confidence is the most attractive quality in a romantic partner. But you know what's legit sexy in everyone? Authenticity.

Confidence can be faked. I think, instead, we should focus on being interested, helpful, and genuine. That way we learn more about who's in the room and how we can be of service, and we're actually more magnetic—which builds real confidence. True confidence is much bigger than personality or day-to-day abilities. It's an unshakeable trust in our own Divinity.

Bless & Release: The desire to be enlightened

Where's the best place for the ego to hide? In personal development workshops.

Bless & Release: Obsessive self-improvement

The shallow parts of self-help culture use fear of failure to motivate people to "overcome" their pain. That's not healing. It's repression.

We're told to cut energy cords, shout our rage into pillows, and set more (and bigger) boundaries. That's not empowerment. It's exhausting.

These "walk away" or "work harder" strategies perpetuate polarization—both inside and outside of us—and ravage our nervous systems. They're too harsh.

You do not need to hyperfocus on "fixing" yourself. When you live from heart intelligence, anything not aligned with that energy falls away. Heavy energies will drop to the side because they can't latch on to the higher vibration.

You're not letting go to become "better." You're letting go to become *lighter*.

You're not proving how well you can manifest. You're getting to know your power.

Bless & Release: Excessive boundaries

Healthy boundaries are part of being a spiritually mature adult. But when we get over-bounded, we block our Life Force and stress our nervous system. There's a difference between boundaries and barriers.

When we're forming a new habit of self-respect, sometimes we overcorrect in the boundary department. Emotional barriers can backfire. We don't need to categorize everything into "what works for me and what doesn't." Life is messy and full of opportunities to choose boundless Love.

Bless & Release: Trying to prove that you're worthy

If one of your children asked you, "Am I worthy of your love?" you'd scoop them up in your arms and say, "What a silly question. You have my love always, no matter what."

You don't need to feel worthy to manifest. A carpenter doesn't need to feel worthy of building a house; he shows up consistently and applies his skill. Manifesting is a metaphysical technology available to anybody, but how you identify—as blessed, qualified, divine, or "unworthy"—influences the creation process.

The heart doesn't ask questions about "worthiness."

The ego talks about it non-stop. *Am I worthy yet? Am I worthy now? Does this make me worthy?* We can spend years hustling to prove we're worthy of what we long for. What a racket.

Worthlessness and worthiness are mirages—neither are true states. Your Soul operates way beyond this duality.

When you feel yourself asking if you're worthy, breathe into your heart and embrace the impulse. Remember: You are pure Radiance. You are the healer. Bring your fear of unworthiness into your heart space and let it relax.

Bless your fear of unworthiness so that your fear of unworthiness doesn't rule you.

Bless & Release: Doing hard things to prove your value

The unhealed part of us is hooked on the process of overcoming. Hardship, guilt, suffering... none of these are requirements for contributing to society. You're still relevant if your life is easy.

Bless & Release: Manifestation fixation

Unpopular opinion: we're not going to get everything we think we want in this lifetime. There's karma to consider, and awakening is a very long game. On the way to our successes, we often discover that what we've been chasing isn't even good for us—and the way we're chasing it isn't good for us either.

Look back on your own life and think about those things you went after and didn't get—and how glad you are now that you *didn't* get them. But how obsessed were we, right?! So obsessed. And then so self-critical because we thought we weren't manifesting right. Worse, a lot of us interpreted those closed doors as punishment.

No matter the circumstances—how much karma someone has to burn or good fortune they're blessed with in this incarnation—connection to the Divine is everybody's birthright. No matter what hand you've been dealt, the only game to play is waking up to your Divinity.

The goal is to become aware of the perpetual embrace of life, where self and other merge, where wanting and being melt together. This is beyond the mind and its manifestation frameworks. This is the Divinity that creates the mind that can become aware of its Divinity!

Transcendental experiences transcend desire. These can happen when you're doing the dishes or sitting with someone in hospice. Making plans, making love, watching your breath, watching the birds.

Whether it's a miraculous recovery or the sweet relief of forgiving someone, blessing moments fill us up and wash away delusions.

After an awakened moment, we step back into the matrix wanting less, because we just merged with The All. Then our vision boards might seem a little hokey. And all the reasons we gave ourselves for being behind or not enough... so silly.

Bless it all.

There's a divine twist in all of this. When we let go of illusory limitations and the stories we've outgrown, we realize that we can manifest a whole new world.

Bless & Release: What went wrong

There's a New Age platitude that says, "There's no such thing as a mistake." That's half-mistaken. We can leave before the miracle happens. We can let our wounded self choose people we think will heal us. We can cause harm. We can hold on too long. And we know it.

Buddhism teaches that there is Right Speech, Right Action, and Right Livelihood. Which means a lot can go wrong.

And yet! All the shades of right and wrong are part of the human curriculum.

We learn through mistakes.

We graduate when we bless them.

Bless & Release: Your self-judgment about being judgmental

I try my best to practice what I preach—it's good for business. I've studied karma, and cause and effect, and I know I don't want the vibes of being a Judge Judy, and yet...

I'm judgin' everybody all the time. Y'all could be much further along, don't ya think?

It happens; I slip into judgment. *They should have just done what I told them to do,* I can't help but think. *That should be pretty obvious. I'm right, and I'm okay with being right. They got themselves into this.*

Then the guilt hits. *Eeshk, Danielle. This is cursing, not blessing. You've been silly and defiant before. And you know this is not good energy. This will come back on you. You need to be more Buddhist, and patient, and unconditional, and enlightened, and on brand.*

And just like that, I'm judging myself for being judgmental.

This is interesting terrain because personalities—which are mental constructs—are innately judgmental. We all have preferences we use to navigate life, choosing right and wrong, better and worse...

Judgment is a very human propensity. The question is: How do we use that judgment? As insight into our own shadow or others', or both? As a weapon or an invitation?

When you judge yourself for being judgmental, you become *more* judgmental. That's what focused *negative* intention does. This means this is actually a great opportunity to practice self-compassion, which inevitably ripples outward to others.

Bring Judge Joe and all that guilt and worry about karma into your heart and let it rest. It's part of you. When we orient towards the Soul, we can notice the judgy behaviour and let it pass through. When we're kind to our judgments, we become less judgmental.

Bless & Release: The desire to be in control all of the time

You know it's an illusion. Fear tries to convince us that if we let go of control, everything will fall apart. But it's the opposite. When we stop trying to force everything, Truth and Joy start to fall into place.

Bless & Release: The unspoken vow that you need to do it all by yourself

Years ago, I sent a group text to my besties, "I'm on the verge. Can you send prayers up, light a candle, whatever feels right." They knew what I was praying for. I sent an obnoxious chain of hugs and kisses for effect.

Immediately, every friend responded, *Done! Doing it! Holding you in the Light! I love you! You got this!* One friend texted a photo of the candle she lit and the sacred object she placed on her altar for me. And she said, "It's an honour to help you."

And I melted. I'd never thought of it that way.

Most people want to help, but more than that—they cherish the opportunity. Give them the honour.

Bless & Release: Your unmet needs and desires

Did you know that trees stop sending nutrients to their broken branches so that more fruit can grow on the healthy branches? We have to stop feeding what's not working. Unmet needs take up a lot of inner real estate.

I'm a big fan of having funerals for expired dreams.

Here's the eulogy:

It didn't happen. It's not going to happen. Now let's focus on what we can make happen.

If resentment is circling in your energy field, it will repel all kinds of fulfillment and abundance. Resentment is the polar opposite of appreciation. Bless & release it.

Embracing the disappointment and grief of our unmet needs (and this includes everything related to our parents and exes) frees up energy to be grateful for what we have and to create new realities. When we let go of our disappointments, our real-time needs are more likely to be met—in ways that exceed our expectations.

Bless & Release: Your worry

> *Who of you by worrying can add a single hour to your life?*
> —Luke 12:25

Worry is a very dense, heavy energy. It comes from the disorganized part of the mind. Worry depletes the Life Force that's meant to support us. It wears us down.

Worry and concern have different textures. Worry acts helpless. Concern is proactive and alert. Worry obstructs healing. Concern can facilitate it.

The first step to transforming worry (like any other emotion) is to realize that you're not the worry itself. It's simply a visitor in your energy field.

Be compassionate with your worry. See it in your heart, and project some higher, antidotal energies on it. As it basks in light, say or think, *Courage, Divine Order, Trust, Love.* If it acts up, bless it again with your focused positive attention. Then get some rest.

Bless & Release: Unrealistic expectations

Unspoken expectations can become resentment.

Excessive expectations can destabilize relationships and dreams.

Unconscious expectations create inner confusion and outer mixed signals.

We're often unconscious of *what we really want.*

Or we know what we want, but we don't feel worthy of it.

Or we don't trust that life will deliver it.

Expectations, preferences, standards... they're all powerful choice points—if we choose them consciously.

The power move is to become aware of what's behind our expectations. How do we do that?

First, we need to let down our defences and get up close to our expectations to see where they came from. Then we figure out how they make us feel. This requires a calm nervous system and a bit of light work.

Here's what I suggest. Do The Centering Practice with your expectations.

Go for a walk with your top five goals or desires in mind, for example, financial projections, or how you expect your kids or your partner to show up for you, or how you're planning on getting healthier.

Place each expectation, one at a time, into your heart center. Don't pre-judge them as needy, normal, or wise. Just let them come into the light frequencies.

And then notice your emotions. Which expectations feel absurd and clingy? Which ones feel lit up and dignified? Let that light keep pulsing in your heart.

Then wrap it up. You don't need to analyze it further or choose to immediately hit pause or double down on any of your goals. Just watch what happens when you keep blessing your expectations over the next few weeks. Some of them will fall away, like they just changed their mind and are good now. Others will become refined and beautiful parts of your identity. And your identity is key to what you create.

And there we have it: a new way of meeting expectations.

BLESS & RELEASE **DISAPPOINTMENT**
BLESS & RELEASE **GRIEF**
BLESS & RELEASE **RESENTMENT**
ANGER

This list might appear overwhelming, I know, but all of these experiences and emotions are interconnected. Where there's anger in the present, there's usually unresolved grief from the past. If we pull at one thread, we can unravel a lot of energy and emotion that can become transmuted into productive power.

The Disappointment-To-Anger Sequence:

1. Unmet needs lead to **disappointment**.
2. Disappointment gives rise to **grief.**
3. Unresolved grief turns into **resentment**.
4. Holding on to resentment creates **anger**.

All of these energies can find resolution with focused positive intention—blessing.

Disappointment into grief

First comes the disappointment of unmet needs. Welcome to Earth! This is a natural predicament, since we're all humans learning how to heal ourselves and each other—most specifically, through relationships.

There's a 100% likelihood that, to varying degrees, we will all feel unseen, unheard, or not loved in the ways that we want to be. Maybe this makes you feel like we're all in this together or totally bereft, but the experience of unmet needs is something we all have in common.

When we're children, we aren't able to fully process not having our needs met. This can start in infancy or on the first day of kindergarten. Regardless of when it happens, the implicit grief that comes from unmet needs registers in our energy field. And we haul it around until we're mature enough to process it on our own or can afford therapy. Whichever comes first.

Eventually, when we're more energetically robust and wiser, and have the psychological fortitude, we can process the disappointment and grief. If we choose to. May we choose to.

Grief into resentment

If we don't treat our grief with compassion, it thickens into resentment over time. Resentment can be a little cranky, or it can be seething.

Resentment is one of the root causes of cynicism and doubt. It causes us to hoard resources out of fear of lack or future disappointment. It makes us guarded.

Resentment is a huge obstacle to abundance in all forms—love, success, comfort, friendship. Holding on to our unmet needs perpetuates not having our needs met in the present. It becomes a vicious cycle of chasing and not receiving. Working harder to get our needs met creates a repulsion effect in our magnetic field.

Resentment into anger

Now imagine what blessing work could do for this grief.

We bring a specific resentment or complaint into the heart, and instead of judging it, we witness it. Love it. Knowing we're in a safe place now. We take a few steady breaths and allow the rainbow spectrum of light to gently loosen the resentment. We soften resentfulness and create space for sadness.

Now imagine if we never did this work. We're resentful about this and that, so many things. What started as heartbreak and crankiness about not getting what we want becomes so dense and heavy that it sinks into anger.

Many people spend a lifetime in this space.

Anger into healing

Maybe we get a life coach or find a church. We join a program with "steps" or modules. We meditate. In all earnestness, we try to be a more loving person by finally dealing with our anger.

We ask our anger to behave. We try to transform it with patience or gratitude. We tell it that it has no right to exist (as if that will make it go away).

Unconsciously, we curse our anger, rather than heal it.

You may believe that you would be a better person without your anger. More lovable. More worthy of... having your needs met.

But, baby, if you fight your anger, it will fight you right back. It's looking to be seen, heard, loved. Bless it, and it will stop acting out.

What we embrace transforms—and makes us more loving.

Bless & Release: Trying to convince others that you're right (and they're wrong)

The ego wants validation. The heart wants to get on with living. When you feel compelled to convince someone of anything, breathe into your heart, and bless your impatience and desire to be right.

Bless & Release: The idea that because you were wrong, you don't belong

We're going to get it wrong. We learn and grow through contrast. Making mistakes doesn't mean that you don't belong at the table.

Bless & Release: Your fear of rejection

I think rejection is one of the most painful parts of being human. We all deal with rejection in various forms: being dismissed, silenced, or invalidated. Often, it can be traced back to a childhood wound that has become adaptive: a theme that keeps showing up in adulthood. In this sense, rejection could be considered one of the root causes of trauma.

When we're rejected as children for who we are, we grow up looking for proof in the world that we're not wanted or worthy of Acceptance.

At the same time, we work really hard not to be rejected. We perform. Fawn. Mask. Go quiet. Get louder. And not-so-ironically, we end up feeling like no one knows the *real* us.

The fear of rejection stays active in our energy field and plays out in relationships. You may win the Pulitzer, but your brother still hasn't read your book. Your crush lost interest when you told them about the New World Order. You launched something you're proud of, but it didn't get the clicks. Somehow, you can't seem to get the thing you want most.

Eventually, the rejection pain intensifies until you're fed up. And then, you see the pattern:

You've spent your life trying not to be rejected. "Don't get rejected" has become your survival strategy. And that fear has created more of the same.

Healing begins when you give yourself what you've been seeking all along: Acceptance. You breathe into your heart. You bring in the pain, and while it can feel gross, it's energizing at the same time. And there, right next to your rejection phobia, you see something else:

The most sublimely beautiful desire to be loved for who you are.

You bring it into your heart, and the vibration is raised.

Then you release it back into your energy field, lighter.

Chapter 5

Reframing problems

There is nothing either good or bad, but thinking makes it so.
—William Shakespeare, *Hamlet*

Whether something is a problem or an opportunity depends on how you look at it.

Life is full of what we could call problems. Old problems. And new problems that we tend to treat like the old problems. Problem handling is its own paradigm, one we can either get stuck in or learn to master.

Problems don't change until you change how you relate to them.

This is an invitation **to begin to relate differently—more powerfully and more spiritually—to everything we've been conditioned to resist and discard.**

Bless or stress?

When a challenge shows up, a Super Blesser asks:

How big of a problem do I want to make this?

The obvious answer is always, "Not that big of a problem."

Bless? Or stress?

On the problem scale of mildly inconvenienced to histrionic, where do you want to rank? Because it's all perspective.

We can't control most circumstances in our lives, but we *can* choose how we *think* about them.

When we look at babies, sunsets, or the Fibonacci sequence, we think, "The Creator makes perfection!" But somehow our challenges seem to fall outside of that cosmic tapestry. If storms and fires are the work of the Divine, so are flat tires and breakups. All are blessings in disguise.

Problems become portals when we get excited about transforming them. Where everyone else sees a roadblock, we can be like, "Guys! It's a secret passage to Higher Consciousness!"

We often assume every "problem" needs to be solved with a mental strategy—a tactic, a game plan, an objective. And sometimes it is that straightforward. Money needs to be managed. Families need schedules. Emergencies happen. But when you choose to embrace rather than push back, you're working with the Higher Mind, and your perception begins to shift.

You'll stop seeing so many things as problems to begin with.

I'm not talking about ocean pollution or moral decline, but the emotional, perceptual stuff—the things we think we need to give our energy to—*but we really don't.* Like: What people think of us. Who agrees with us. What anyone does with their own money. Who's right and who's wrong. What celebrities do on weekends. The size of our butts. Who's not following the rules (that keep changing anyway).

To paraphrase the philosopher Marcus Aurelius, "You always have the power to have no opinion."

Most inconveniences and many disappointments can be re-categorized as non-problems. It's our emotions—more specifically, *our reactions* to our emotions—that can be *problematic.*

When we defuse our emotions, we defuse the problem.

How do we do that? Well, it's not as clinical as it might sound. It's not a heartless procedure. In fact, it's a very heart-full process.

We defuse our emotions by being curious and compassionate with them.

This is loving detachment. What the Buddha was getting at with the practice of detachment is: a lot of the sh*t that used to matter to you... just won't anymore.

As your mind brightens (literally) with kindness and optimism, you'll see "problems" very differently.

Instead of privileging our freakouts or yelling back at our anger, we take charge of our emotions and show them love and respect. Instead of reacting to our reactions, we get still. And the discomfort that arises? We bring it into our hearts. Blessing discomfort is a very grown-up move.

We see ourselves as the healer, not the wound. Instead of focusing on what to be angry or disappointed about, we focus on our capacity to circulate energy. We do it with our breath, our attention, our visualization. Getting centered. Blessing it and releasing it back into our energy field. Reducing the size of the problem.

This is heart-mind coherence.

The more we're able to neutralize our emotionality, the faster the ick from an argument will rinse away. The more compassionate we are with our rage or disappointment, the sooner the emotional inflammation cools down. When we can have a relaxed dialogue with our confusion and fear, we stay in our bodies, instead of disassociating.

You're going to be so amazing at this new way of life. You'll DM me and say, "Holiday dinner with my family used to set me OFF. Now I just bless those muthers. Way better!"

When you're a Super Blesser, other people's opinions aren't that much of a problem.

Problem reframing is evolutionary

> *The world is you; you are the problem;*
> *the problem is not separate from you;*
> *the world is a projection of yourself.*
> —J. Krishnamurti, *The First and Last Freedom*

When we question if a change, challenge, or disappointment is truly a problem, we're entering the territory of the Higher Mind. This is exciting!

Definitions are meant to delineate. That's what the mind does so well. But they can also limit where our Life Force flows. Defining something—or someone—as "not like me," "foreign to me and therefore threatening," "superior," "inferior," or "other" can become a form of restriction.

When we *redefine* problems, however, we're flirting with non-dualism—unity consciousness. We stop labelling everything that happens as either good or bad, positive or negative. We stop categorizing people as useful to us or not, worthy of our love or... pass.

When we make conscious choices for the good of all, we're tapping into Oneness consciousness. We become more aware that all life flows from the same Source. All colours come from pure light. All experiences emerge from the same Life Force. It's all related.

From this perspective, we don't need to put our pain in a box and call it negative. That doesn't mean it's not heavy, but we can choose to carry our pain lightly.

We begin to see that whatever comes into our life is Life Force taking form, even if it's the form of pain or of happiness. We're having a sensory experience of the forms that come from the great formlessness.

This is what it means to be alive: sensing!

Pain, then, can be defined as a sensation. Simply that. Happiness, too: a sensation. Disappointment, victory, courage... all sensations from the Divine that help you become aware of your greater aliveness and your Divinity.

We can treat all feelings and experiences—and people—as opportunities to be more loving, more aware, and more alive!

With every sensation that we bless and bring into our heart, we strengthen our connection to the field of unified consciousness. The act of blessing—of loving recognition—gives us access to Truth.

Chapter 6

Physics has a crush on spirituality

If you want to find the secrets of the universe,
think in terms of energy, frequency, and vibration.
—Nikola Tesla

Spiritual truths are natural laws. They're not just beliefs. For the nerds, the logicians, *and* my homey metaphysicians: every major spiritual principle I share has a scientific counterpart. These aren't loose correlations. Measurable, peer-reviewed research now syncs with ancient traditions, Egyptian mystery schools *and* advances in brain health, yogic mastery *and* neuroplasticity.

So let's get metaphysical...

The physics of letting go & manifesting (aka the science of love and light)

1. **Everything is a form of energy.** Everything in this universe is made up of light and chemical elements. Trees, animals, cells. Minerals, colours, clouds. Thoughts, feelings, intentions. Actions, beliefs, touch. Conversations. Relationships. You.

2. **Everything has its own energy field.** These electromagnetic fields are penetrable and capable of penetrating. Your personal field is like your wi-fi of aliveness—and the strength of your signal depends on your energy flow.

3. **Energy cannot be created or destroyed; it can only be transformed.** We can't make something that exists disappear. There are no takebacks, but there can be major upgrades. We can transform anything and everything—including our current state, and therefore, our reality—into a higher state. Focused positive intention, blessing, is alchemy.

   This is the first law of thermodynamics, also known as the law of conservation of energy. (I love this term. I'm going to use it to get out of social functions. "Friday? Can't make it. I'm practicing the law of conservation of energy.")

4. **Everything in the universe is in constant motion—and has its own vibration.** This is the principle of vibration. Spirit (energy) exists at one end of the pole of motion, and matter at the other end. Between the two poles are millions of different rates of vibration.

Thoughts and words are vibrations. Rocks, chairs, rivers, and artwork vibrate. Everything in the universe has its own vibrational pace—slow to lightspeed, stuck to flowing.

5. **Like attracts like.** This is the law of manifestation.

   Vibrations attract similar vibrations—everything in the universe likes to get on the same wavelength. Life Force favours harmony.

   We attract experiences that correspond to our vibration—to what's in our energy field. Change the contents of your energy field—your thoughts, words, and actions—and you shift what you experience.

6. **Energy follows thought.** The energy radiating from your brain and heart is physically measurable. Since like attracts like, the most powerful questions to ask yourself are, "What's the energy of the thoughts I'm thinking?" and "Do I want more or less of that energy?"

7. **Energy naturally moves in a circulatory way.** Think: energy vortices, water swirling, planetary orbits, inhaling and exhaling. All cycles. Right now, you're in the center of your own energy field, *circulating light from your heart center!*

   Energy can change form—becoming denser or lighter—through consuming and composting. Receiving and giving. Blessing & releasing.

8. **Everything is always changing.** Nothing in the known universe stays the same.

   When we resist change, we fight the flow of universal intelligence—and that causes suffering. Don't feed what hurts you. When we feed energies that hurt us, we add to our suffering.

9. **All energy comes from, and returns to, the pure life Source—** inextinguishable Light!

   All colours—red, orange, yellow, green, blue, and violet—come from pure white light. And each colour emits a specific vibration of Life Force.

   Happy, sad, mad, glad. Stuck, flowing. Wise, ignorant. All of your expressions and perceptions, whether they are illusion or truth, are tethered to pure Source energy—some might call this the Divine.

10. **We have freewill to use energy however we choose.** Life Force can be used to create or destroy, for better or for worse. May we choose well.

When you know, you know

Understanding the physics of letting go and manifesting doesn't only satisfy the intellect—it validates our intuition.

So many spiritual seekers feel the need to apologize for their perspective: "I know this sounds *woo-woo,* but..." We downplay the power, whispering about metaphysics like we're having an affair. But your Light is legit.

Darling, stop apologizing for having an inside track on how reality works. You're a natural at *quantum physics*. And besides, if you don't speak your truth, how will we find each other?

When you know that heart coherence is measurable, that light visualization shifts your brain waves, and that sending blessings activates your body's healing systems, then you can fully optimize the process.

Ancient mystics were the scientists of their day. Modern physics is catching up to what they always knew:

> **Love transforms everything it comes into contact with.**

Getting centered is not a figure of speech. Blessing is not magical thinking. It's how you work with the fundamental energies of the universe.

Nature lets go to grow

> *What goes too long unchanged destroys itself.*
> *The forest is forever because it dies and dies and so lives.*
> —Ursula K. Le Guin, *Tales from Earthsea*

We are designed to flow, to move, to change. In all ecosystems, holding on to what's expired leads to damage or destruction. **The more nature lets go, the more it grows.**

Get ready for some motivational metaphors.

Volcanoes have small vents that convert energy so that catastrophic eruptions don't happen. Maybe you should have a clearing conversation before there's an outburst.

When a tree has a diseased branch, the entire tree system conspires to stop sending nutrients to that branch so it can die off without affecting the rest of the tree.

Even black holes are always letting go! Black holes are not vortices where everything evaporates. No energy in the universe can be destroyed; it can only be transformed. Black holes are constantly converting mass into energy—a continuous cycle of blessing & releasing.

You're alive because your body is constantly transforming energy. Your nervous system, your heartbeat, your breathing—it's all energy in constant transformation. When we go with the flow, we get farther ahead, faster.

Why this practice works: spiritual principles meet scientific proof

> ***metaphysics.*** noun
> *metaphysica,* from Medieval Greek, "the works after the physics." One of the oldest branches of philosophy, metaphysics examines the structure of reality, existence, time, and space; and the relationship between matter and mind. Aristotle designated metaphysics as the "first philosophy."

THE METAPHYSICS	THE PHYSICS
Energy follows thought. Your thoughts function like magnets in your energy field.	**Electromagnetic field theory & neuroplasticity.** Your brain is an electromagnetic organ. Thoughts create measurable activity. What you focus on repeatedly strengthens those neural pathways—neurons that fire together, wire together.
What you embrace transforms. Healing is integration, not annihilation. Blessing is alchemy.	**The first law of thermodynamics (law of conservation of energy).** Energy cannot be created or destroyed; it can only be transformed. Your body continuously transforms energy through your nervous system, heartbeat, and breath.
What you push away pushes back. Resistance traps energy. Force attracts counterforce.	**Newton's third law.** For every action, there is an equal and opposite reaction. Pushing creates pushback.
Blessing—conscious awareness, heals. Observing something with focused positive intention changes it.	**The observer effect.** Observation changes what's being observed; focused attention creates order in chaotic systems.
Like attracts like. Higher-frequency emotional states naturally sync with and attract matching experiences.	**Frequency resonance.** When two things vibrate at similar frequencies, they amplify each other. Thoughts and emotions carry specific frequencies. Heart coherence produces smooth, ordered waves.
The heart is command central. The heart is the seat of the Soul. When you work from the heart center, you circulate high-frequency energy through all systems.	**Heart-brain communication.** Your heart has 40,000+ neurons that continuously communicate with your brain. Heart coherence synchronizes your entire nervous system. The heart's electromagnetic field is the strongest in the body.

The Centering Practice: the steps and the physics

This is what's happening in your body when you practice centering:

THE STEP	THE PHYSICS
Breathe. Place your right hand on your heart for a few breaths.	Slow breathing stimulates the vagus nerve—your relaxation metre—which shifts you from fight-or-flight into rest-and-digest mode. At about 5-6 breaths per minute, you create heart rate variability (HRV) coherence. Your heart rhythm smooths out. Your brain shifts into alpha and theta states. Stress hormones drop. Feel-good neurotransmitters rise.
Positive thought. Recall a beautiful memory, feeling, or virtue.	Meditative focus interrupts rumination and rewires your brain towards possibility thinking. Uplifting emotions activate the parasympathetic system, calm stress hormones, and signal safety to your body.
Gold light. Imagine warm, golden light filling your heart.	Your visual cortex doesn't distinguish between seeing and imagining colour. Meditators visualizing colour show the same brainwave changes as if viewing actual coloured light. You're training your brain's mirror network in real time.
Bring it into your heart. See what you're healing or manifesting in the center of your heart—as a scene, moment, word, symbol, or thought.	Your heart communicates with your brain through 40,000+ intrinsic neurons, influencing perception and mood. Direct compassionate attention generates electromagnetic coherence measurable several feet from your body. Your focused intention reduces fear-center reactivity and increases soothing-circuit regulation. What you embrace transforms.

THE STEP	THE PHYSICS
Light spectrum. Shine rainbow colours on what you're blessing, like colours moving through stained glass.	Different colours create distinct brainwave patterns. Visualizing healing frequencies (soft pinks, peach tones, golds, minty greens, sky blues, pale purples) shifts your brain into deep relaxation and heightened awareness. Areas associated with empathy and compassion light up. You're bathing your nervous system in healing frequencies.
Add in virtues if you like. Project or speak higher qualities into your heart center: Compassion, Love, Joy, Forgiveness, abundance.	Every thought carries measurable electrical and biochemical activity. Uplifting virtues create smooth, coherent heart rhythms (unlike the chaotic patterns of stress). Repetitive positive focus strengthens neural pathways—neurons that fire together, wire together.
Let what you've blessed relax in your heart. No need to fixate or analyze.	Curiosity and compassion change your perception. The observer effect proves that observing something inevitably changes it. When you've completed the practice, you've deepened your understanding of and connection to what you want to heal or manifest. You're becoming a more conscious creator.

Chapter 7

Your energy field

You are a gluten-free donut of light

Your energy field is your aura. It's also called a torus, the toroidal field. It's often called a donut of light. Which I *love*. **We're all gluten-free donuts of light!**

This is you:

This is you on a good day. And a bad day.

This is you when you're struggling with addictive behaviours. This is you in prayer and in bliss.

You're energy, radiating.

Your energy field is what people feel when you walk into a room. Its reach varies from person to person. Most Yogic teachings say that the average person's energy field extends about 1 to 3 feet from their body. That's like a muggle-sized aura.

Advanced Yogis and spiritual practitioners, people with wizard-sized energy fields, reach about 9 to 12 feet. I've heard that the energetic radius of ascended masters, gurus, and saints can emanate for miles—everyone in the vicinity is blessed within that strong frequency.

The power of our energy field depends, in part, on how "light" and clutter-free it is.

This is why most spiritual practices—meditation, yoga, prayer, bathing and cleansing rituals, saging, offerings—are some form of a purification practice. Living a harmless lifestyle is in and of itself a form of purifying.

The spaciousness, the "lightness," of our energy field depends on what we focus on. Virtues like Generosity and Joy are higher resonance than feelings like shame or criticism. Virtues are luminous. Heavy emotions are cloudy.

When we're practicing love—blessing & releasing—we are actually purifying our energy field until it becomes radiant, strong, and expansive.

Imagine ribbons of light radiating upward from your heart and spouting out the top of your head like a waterfall. The light cascades down your front and back, then returns up through your root chakra. Circulating, looping, the light moves through you.

One more time... Let the light travel up from your heart with each breath, out of your crown chakra, then down the front and back and sides of your body, towards the base of your spine, and up again... and again, without end. How amazing and luminous is that?!

> *Metaphysically speaking, our energy field is the house we live in, despite being unable to 'see' its contents. Our day-to-day experiences and the larger life experiences (birth, death, divorce, perceived failures, endings...) are determined by the quality of frequency, resonance, and the vibration of our field.*
> —V.S.

Einstein taught that "the field is the sole governing agency of the particle." This profound statement about the nature of life can also be applied to metaphysics. Here, "the field" is the electromagnetic field (your aura, your energy field, your donut of light). "The particle" is your physical form/body.

The content of your energy field governs your physical life.

What's in your energy field?

Thoughts, words, and actions. Conscious and unconscious. Intentional and habitual.

Imagine that each of your thoughts is a little orb or magnetic marble, circulating through your energy field. The key word here is *magnetic.*

Now let's say you're on a forest walk. Lush trees, sweet oxygen. And you think to yourself, "I'm sooo grateful for this nature-healing." The energy of that thought is *Gratitude.*

Little "Gratitude magnets" now start to circulate in your energy field. They glide up through your crown chakra where your other thoughts are hanging out, and loop through your body, passing all your organs and chakras.

As they cycle, they send a message to your whole body, drawing even more Gratitude thoughts from the back of your mind. One grateful thought evokes another grateful thought, because like attracts like—this is the law of vibration.

If I were standing next to you, your Gratitude magnets would pass through my energy field too.

Thank you.

Whatever is in your energy field magnetizes more of the same into your radius.

Negative feelings are just as magnetic, of course. And because like attracts like and misery loves company, one negative word can stir up more negative thoughts from the back of your mind or from the person you're talking to. Thoughts of the same vibration cluster, like clouds accumulating.

Here's a sobering metaphysical principle: Every thought you've ever had and word you've spoken—the energy of everything you've ever done—remains in your energy field indefinitely. **We can choose to shift the energy.**

Whatever you consciously focus on will create a shift in your auric field. We can work to raise the energy frequency of what we carry around—lightening our load through our spiritual practices.

One light, many names

Many cultures reference the energy field:

- Tibetan Buddhism refers to it as the Aura of Light.
- Yogic teachings call it the Auric Egg.
- Kabbalists call it Ohr Makif.
- Ancient Romans referred to it as Aureola.
- Ancient Persia called it Farr, or ***Khvarenah.***
- The mathematician Pythagoras called it the luminous body.
- Rosicrucian philosophers call it the Soul Body.
- Theosophy calls it the auric envelope.
- Hinduism calls it Pranamaya Kosha.
- The Native American people, the Navajo, call it Shá́ńdíín.
- Polynesia… Mana. Japan… Ki. China… Wei Qi.

Our energy bubbles bumpin'

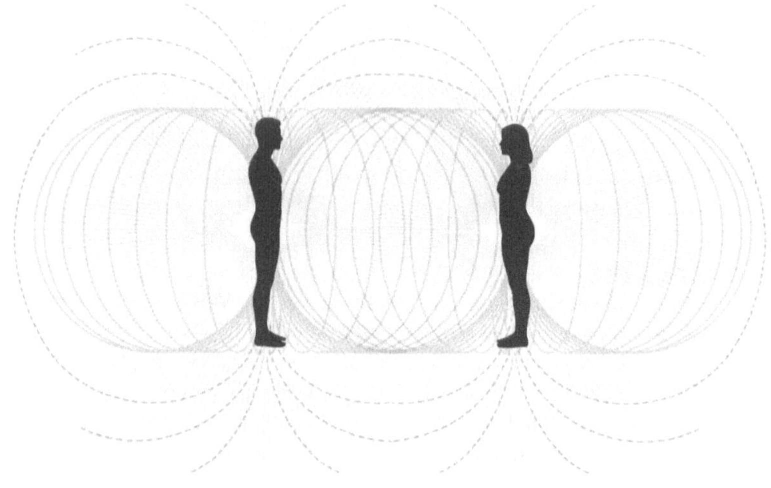

See the God in everyone.
"Everyone" leaves no one out
and everything besides love is cowardice
You wanna be brave, you wanna be tough?
Peace and love is the toughest, hardest thing you can do.
—Flea

All energy fields, including yours, are fueled by the great power grid of the universe—Life Force, prana, chi.

Your energy field is always interacting with everyone else's energy field. That includes minerals, plants, animals, and your neighbours.

We're all just gluten-free donuts of light—merging, triggering, comforting, collaborating, activating, energizing, healing. Blessing.

Really, our *primary job* as human beings is to keep our energy field as uncluttered and as harmless as possible. *Primum non nocere.* First, do no harm. That's our oath of Higher Consciousness.

Once energy particles interact, they can become linked forever—no matter how close or far apart the particles are. When scientists split up entangled particles and put them in laboratories miles apart, the particles behave in the same way, like twins with the same mannerisms.

Humans are made of those same energy particles, and in terms of consciousness, physical distance is irrelevant. Ancients and sages knew this thousands of years before Western science could articulate it. Every mother, lover, and Reiki practitioner knows this.

In physics, it's called quantum entanglement. In psychology, we might call it enmeshment. I think it's our deepest longing: to love and be loved.

Vibes and tribes

So if you hang out with someone who's depressed or resentful, do you "absorb" their heavier energy? Is it really possible for someone to "drain your energy"?

Yes. We're influenced by each other's energy frequencies. Other people's moods can "rub off on us," so to speak. This doesn't mean that we should protect ourselves from people who are suffering—that would make for a lonely existence.

The objective, instead, is to become so radiant and full of love, so compassionate and joyful, that we're more impervious to heavier vibrations. When we're acclimating to the Light and Higher

Consciousness, negative energies fall away—they have nothing to latch onto. No energy match, no energy latch.

We become the positive change agent in every situation.

Chapter 8

How the heart and ego do life

The higher perspective

Let's break down human existence. Easy!

You are a Soul, and you have a mind.

Your Soul is your True Nature, your all-encompassing vastness.

Your mind has two levels:

- Higher Mind, also known as the Universal Mind
- Lower Mind, the home of the ego

Before we go further, let me say this: The Lower Mind is not the villain in our story. It's a key character to move the plot forward. Our shadow is a reflection of the Light. Our suffering leads back to the Light, as does our ignorance. Beauty, brilliance... all of it arises from the same Source.

It's all connected and essential.

As individuals, we may be moving through this evolutionary spiral at different points, yet we're all fundamentally equal. Conscious creation comes with responsibilities, but none of that involves more judgment about our own humanity.

As we identify more with the Soul and realize our vastness, our detachment lessens. The suffering we experience decreases.

The ethos of blessing is to show reverence to all dimensions of ourselves.

- **You are the Soul, the Higher Self.** You could also refer to your Soul as the heart. I'll use both terms.

  The Soul is limitless Love. It is spacious enough to hold all experiences within—with loving discernment. It rejects nothing; everything that arises is observed with compassion. The heart lets everything be *as it is.* It has the time (eternity) and the space (unlimited) to let all types of energies—from people and experiences—emerge and evolve.

  The Soul is unlimited. The mind, however, is linear. It can't comprehend the limitless nature of the Soul. But that's fine; we don't need to fully understand the Soul for it to help us navigate our lives. We leave room for mystery while we keep seeking to know our True Nature.

- **The Soul uses the mind to manifest!** It's like the Soul is the force of nature that directs the mind to make the weather. Pure life energy comes from the heart—the mind harnesses that chi to produce forms and outcomes.

- **The mind is a tool for creating structures and realities.** The Soul uses the mind to envision, perceive, understand, and make connections.

  Here's a pro manifestation tip: Use practices (like The Centering Practice, meditation, prayer, kindness, conscious breathing...) to build a stronger connection to your Soul. The Soul will fill your mind with higher vibration thoughts, which help create Right Action and desired outcomes.

  With devotion and practice, the Light of your Soul will shine through your mind more clearly. Intuition, flashes of insight, Higher Guidance... this is the Soul giving us clear seeing, so that we can take clear action.

  The Higher Mind and the Lower Mind are like having a sharp, elegant tool and a duller instrument at your disposal—both can be used for building, with different levels of ease, effort, and outcomes.

- **The Higher Mind,** also known as the Universal Mind or heart intelligence, is like an infinite library that we all have access to. It's the virtue bank of Wisdom. Our Higher Mind sees things clearly.

  Accessing the Higher Mind feels revelatory and peaceful. Its guidance isn't always easy to follow—it might require us to let go or speak up—but we are at peace with choices made by the Higher Mind.

  The Higher Mind is loving and inclusive, always factoring in the highest good for everyone and everything involved. It's how you know the difference between a wise and an unwise choice. Wise choices always consider the benefit or harm to all beings. If a choice doesn't take all players into loving consideration, it's not a wise choice.

The Higher Mind delivers the wisdom and solutions that ultimately lead to goodness and growth—in other words, progress.

Every time we bless a situation, an emotion, or another being, we gain greater access to the Higher Mind. Every time we withhold love or wish ill, we create a barrier to the Higher Mind.

- **The Lower Mind** is where our capacity to delineate and discriminate comes from. These are very useful capacities, for sure, but balance is key.

  The Lower Mind is not as spacious or inclusive as the Higher Mind. Where the Higher Mind expands and amplifies, the Lower Mind contracts and closes.

  The ego is like a splinter or shard in the Lower Mind. It's a small, limited, bounded point of view. Emphasis on *limited.* The ego can't perceive the larger perspective of life or unified reality—Truth with a capital T. It just doesn't see that clearly. It's not "whole" on its own.

  Because the ego can't see the larger perspective of Oneness and Truth, it "thinks" that it's disconnected and solitary. So it defaults to judging, dividing, ranking, grading, and measuring—perpetuating separateness, which leads to suffering.

Too much of this "thinking" can actually block the Higher Mind. That illusion of apartness and aloneness can eclipse the Soul's Light from entering.

The unconscious wants to become conscious at all times.

The Lower Mind wants to be uplifted.

The homeless parts of ourselves want to go home.

EGO CENTERED...	HEART CENTERED...
These are all interchangeable terms: The ego self. The Lower Mind. Small self. Unhealed self. Shadow self. Abandoned self. Fragmented parts. Personality. Unconscious content. Unconscious mind.	Also interchangeable terms: The heart center. Soul. The Higher Self. Life Force. Prana. Divine Nature. True Nature. Unified self. Non-self. Beyond self. Anima. Essential nature. True being. The Light of Love. Essence. Ka. Atman. Core being. Intuitive self. Eternal self. Inner Wisdom. Divine Light. Divine Love. Divine Power.

Everything is energy, and energy is always in motion: heavy or light, dense or fluid, slow or fast. Imagine energy moving along a pole of vibration, sometimes flowing freely, sometimes getting stuck.

The ego, our "small" self, hangs out at the low-vibration end of the pole. The heart, the Higher Self, vibrates much *higher.*

Truth is high frequency. Illusion is low frequency.

The ego's view is limited. The ego mind perceives its "self" as separate from Life Force, even though that point of view couldn't be (literally) further from the Truth.

The Lower Mind doesn't integrate multiple perspectives or let go easily. The ego's habit is to compartmentalize, contract, and cling.

The heart vibrates at a much higher level, closer to Truth. The heart space is expansive and inclusive. It naturally magnetizes and integrates all energies into its field—no rejection, only welcoming.

Our ego is not the enemy

When the Lower Mind is full of heavy thoughts, beliefs, and opinions, mental and energetic processing lags. Our ego begins to see only in black and white. Overthinking mutes possibilities. Preferences become fewer and more fixed. The personality becomes very predictable and habitual. *This is natural. This is how we grow.*

Our ego sees life through a cracked lens. The more we use it as our filter, the more personality identifications we'll hold—stronger opinions, sharper distinctions, and ideas that separate us from each other. *This is natural. This is how we grow.*

The part of you that's stressed out wants control and to feel safe. Remember, our ego thinks it's separate from the Divine, so it will try to reinforce that false belief. Its strategies to gain greater control will get in the way of actual solutions. And that stifles energy, which is the opposite effect of blessing. *This is natural. This is how we grow.*

I know it might sound like it, but our ego is *not* the enemy. *Unless you treat it like it is.* It's one of our greatest teachers. After all, it's one of our creations.

All of our judgmental thoughts, inferiority struggles, delusions of superiority, and fears cause suffering. *This is natural. This is how we grow.* And eventually this suffering evokes compassion. We cannot build Wisdom without passing through ignorance.

In this way, the Lower Mind is the causeway to the Higher Mind.

Our ego returns us to the heart.

It's a beautiful irony.

As we start seeking greater and more frequent access to the Higher Mind, we find more harmony, which I believe is our deepest craving. At its highest vibration, the mind creates beauty and magnificence—union. What we've thought was a curse brings us to our greatest blessings.

Blessing the part of you that resists love

Sometimes our mind is doing its high-vibe thing. Sometimes, it's doing its low-vibe thing. Sometimes it's loving, sometimes it's ego-ing. Our ego is not separate from us; it's a behavioural pattern.

I've known so many committed spiritual practitioners who have tried to put their ego in its place (*hi, that was me!*), which is the biggest spiritual bypass of them all.

Because the spiritual path is about integrating our desires and aversions—with Love.

Inevitably, our identity and attachments will be challenged. Maybe our pastor or guru gets called out. Perhaps our community begins to unravel. Or our Inner Child tries to get our attention with a panic attack when we least expect it (which is almost always). There's loss, divorce, a choice to get sober...

All these very human, humbling, and life-altering challenges are the Soul's way of getting us to enroll in bless & release bootcamp.

When my friend's home was destroyed by fire, it spurred them to let go of a lifestyle weighed down with a garage full of things they never used and jobs they didn't adore. They moved to the jungle, kept their kids out of conventional schooling, landed remote jobs, and got off all their stress and sleeping meds. The house was gone. Old identities gone. In their place: happiness and meaningfulness they'd never planned for.

How many friends do you have whose bankrupted business or "failed" relationship cleared the way to success or the love of their lives? All of which came after a heap of hurt, loss, and humiliation.

After the universe flattens us, we expand. *If* we choose to. Fires are beyond our control, but rising from the flames is always a choice.

When we let go of our judgments of right and wrong, spiritual or not spiritual, even desirable or repulsive, the Soul drops in with Wisdom and illumination. Loving awareness fills the space that our identities and attachments used to occupy.

We integrate parts of our Lower Mind into our Higher Mind. And we let go of trying to *om* our ego into submission or motivate our feelings to perform better. We make the most enlightened declaration yet: "I have an ego. And I love it."

The mind and the body

A friend of a friend came to me for some spiritual direction about her cancer diagnosis. "Don't fight the cancer," I suggested. "Love it."

She exhaled. "That's what I want to do, but everyone is using language like, 'Fight it, kill it!' But you know, I'm not *angry*. I just want to live."

Yesss.

Whatever therapy you choose, do it from your creative power. "Fighting death" increases the battle in your energy field. "Loving life" fills you with pure Life Force.

Heaps of research connects emotional repression to chronic illness. Illness is a congested emotion, often unexpressed pain calling for our attention.

And we know that using breath, light frequencies, and focused attention transforms the state of negative or suppressed emotions—and our immune systems.

We might think, *Won't the illness stick around if it's getting all this great love from us?* No, babe. Life Force always wants to harmonize.

The energy trapped within the illness wants to be freed.

The heart is your home base

Your Soul is your safe space. Your own heart center offers a deeper safety than therapy, relationships, or any healing modality, ever. Come as you are—busted and brilliant. There's zero judgment in the Soul realm. No matter what you bring into your heart, you will never be told that you eff'd up, that you're behind, or that you don't belong.

The heart is eternal Divine Love. Unconditional Acceptance. There's no better place in the universe to call home.

Think of it this way: The heart space is open and attractive—like a magnet. Your woundedness and pain are like metal filaments—they get pulled into the heart's vortex. There is no push/pull. No examination or possibility of rejection. Only immediate and full Acceptance—the fiercest kind of Compassion.

Mama Soul wants what you've got. Bring her everything. Introduce your fears, your friends, and your most precious future visions. She's vast. Infinite. There's room for everything in the kingdom of the heart space: Love, shame, hate, exhaustion, ecstasy, regrets, unmet needs, Divine Union, bliss. *All of it.*

How does the heart let go? It doesn't have to.
It includes—and loves—everything.

How does the ego let go? It doesn't. It clings and categorizes.

Conscious letting go is integration, and integration happens in the heart because it is pure consciousness: Divine Light, Divine Love, and Divine Power.

Integration is a Soul activity. It arises from a refined motivation that only the heart can hold. The ego can't let go and integrate. Only the Soul is willing and able to embrace all of our unconscious forces.

Are you willing to give over one painful experience—and the suffering that came with it—to the Light of your Soul? Just one. How about one more? And then another? Will you allow the heart to perform its function: to accept and love each experience?

Emotions and thoughts are neutralized in the heart because they are welcomed without judgment.

The heart welcomes what the ego rejects.

The heart brain

The heart has the strongest electromagnetic energy in the body—by far. As a result, researchers have given the anatomical heart a title upgrade: the "heart brain." This is a paradigm shift equivalent to when Galileo declared that the Earth revolved around the sun, not the other way around.

For years, the medical industry taught that the brain pulled the levers for all bodily functions. And that's accurate. But what's directing the brain? It turns out that it's the heart!

The heart has 40,000+ neurons—that is some serious processing power. Your heart actually "thinks," sending cues to the brain *and* most of our major organs, *and* our hormonal system, *and* our nervous system. Of all the messages sent between the heart and the brain, 80% of those signals travel *from the heart to the brain.* Only 20% of the cues originate in the brain.

Researchers at The Heart Math Institute hooked electrocardiogram monitors to people to measure their energy frequency. They found that the heart's electrical field is about 60 times greater in amplitude than the brain's electrical field. So, if the brain's energy registers at, say, 10, the heart's energy tips 600! The heart rules. Literally.

In the traditional 7 chakra system, there are 3 chakras above the heart and 3 chakras below the heart chakra. The heart chakra is the fulcrum of your energy field. Most eastern mystical traditions regard the heart chakra as the center of human consciousness—the seat of the Soul. It's believed to be the best place to concentrate on during meditation.

> *The heart chakra is a vortex that allows us entry into Higher consciousness—the space beyond polarity, of all expansive inclusiveness. This space is vaster than the sky, with no beginning or end.*
> *We're not trying to envision everything "fitting into" the heart vortex. Our awareness is much more expanded.*
> *We work with the heart chakra so as to identify as the Soul.*
> *We're working with the truth of our infinite nature.*
> —V.S.

The heart chakra is the portal to Divine Love and all other virtues. It's the gateway to your Higher Self. I can't overstate the significance of this.

The heart chakra is a doorway within your etheric body that leads to Higher Consciousness.

Knock knock? Who's there? INFINITY!

Chapter 9

Conditioned to cling

Everything I've ever let go of has claw marks on it.
—David Foster Wallace, *Infinite Jest*

The faux let go

The breakup. I drove 6 hours from New Mexico to get across the Texas state line, so I could leave torn-up love letters from an ex-boyfriend in another state. I pulled over to the side of the road, hiked to the tallest cactus, and cast his notes to the wind, like microaggression confetti.

The ritual was satisfying, but my co-pilot girlfriend had to listen to me go on and on about the ex for the 6-hour drive back home. *Weren't you supposed to let go of that dawg in Texas?*

The firing. I was ousted from a business I had co-founded due to "creative differences" with the CEO we had hired. They dismissed me in a Starbucks, presumably so I wouldn't make a scene. Driving home, I rolled up the car windows, white-knuckled the steering wheel, and screamed. And screamed. I made a scene alright.

Was it useful? Nah. My anger stayed heavy in my gut. I just felt utterly drained. And slightly embarrassed at whoever saw me in hysterics on the parkway.

The boundaries. I incanted Archangel Michael prayers to help cut cords with a boss who had bad-boy boundaries. I paced San Francisco in the rain, visualizing electric blue swords severing our karmic connection. I added lightsaber sounds for effect. Then, I went to work on Monday, acting like the kiss never happened.

My letting-go rituals were more like rebellions.

While they *did* help quell obsessing over the people involved, I held on to the same *patterns of relating.* Which is what I really needed to bless & release.

I was frantically trying to get rid of the hurt instead of sitting with it and learning what it could teach me. My bruised ego wanted to place blame. I wanted distance from *the pressure of discomfort.*

I needed to meet both the betrayals and my weaknesses with gentleness. That was the biggest learning.

There's a natural order to letting go effectively. First, the heart does the healing. Then, rituals seal the deal.

When we bless & release, we're not necessarily letting go of people, places, or situations—we can keep those. What we're releasing is our attachments to the ideas and energies that restrict us. We're letting go of our limiting thinking and limiting beliefs. *We're learning to suffer less.*

Then it's a beautiful domino effect. The limits go, we feel more spacious, and finally, more Love pours into us. It's what Buddhists call Bodhichitta, *the mind of awakening*. What awakens the mind is Love!

Effective letting go isn't "the art of not giving a f*ck."

It's the opposite. Effective letting go is less *f*ck it*, more *love it*.

The cling is cultural

Humans tend to cling. We even cling to things that are already sinking. We've been conditioned to accumulate, to grasp, to hold our ground—which usually means holding on to the past.

The cling is partly cultural. We're told to get a job, get power, get stuff, get better, get more. Then get storage for all that we've got—some of which we're still paying for. Get approval, even from people we don't even know. Get love, even from people who don't really love themselves. Get it in writing. And if it hurts, get a pill so we can just get on with it.

And we're told to keep it because we might need it. Keep our regrets so we don't repeat the same mistakes. Keep our secrets so we can keep up appearances. And if we still don't feel like we belong, just keep trying. We'll get there if we keep at it.

We hear heaps more messaging about getting, keeping, and conquering than we do about resolving, forgiving, and surrendering.

Blessing & releasing is counterculture.

It might even *seem counterintuitive.* But it isn't. We're perfectly designed to compost physical and energetic matter into nutrients so we can flourish in even the harshest conditions.

Our bodies are in a perpetual flow of receiving and releasing. So is nature. All forms of success—health, wealth, relationships, creativity—are the result of intentionally circulating energy.

A healthy life depends on letting go.

Chapter 10

What do you want to let go of?

I WANT TO LET GO OF...

Self-shaming patterns and judgment. The story that my worth and value come from being productive and having a clear direction. The idea that I have to be fully healed, super enlightened, "complete," to be whole or to demonstrate the work. My lack of ambition, feeling guilty about not going home for a family vacation, my insecurity around people who make more money than I do, feeling like I'm behind in life. Expectations of myself and others. Managing others. Results. Being affected by others. Being overpowered by others. Fear of public speaking. Regrets and guilt related to parenting. Overthinking. Proving my worth. Obligations. Old self, old roles, old masks. Too much responsibility. Self-hate. Negativity. Resentment. Self-abandonment. Worry. Hustle. The pain of infertility. Unknown attachments. Self-doubt and fear. Looping thoughts. Trauma. Shame of debt. Being "allowed." Perfectionism. Disappointments. Physical pain and ailments. Pretending to be someone else. Being judged or not accepted. Relationships that don't serve me anymore. Being right. Getting it right. Not trusting myself or my instincts. Abandonment and rejection. Anger. Tension. Resisting my passion.

When we survey people about what they want to let go of, their answers are peppered with phrases like, "Despite all my work...," "Again and again...," and "I'm still trying to..."

We're frustrated with slow progress. We seem to be ashamed of not being "healed" yet. We have a sense of urgency around letting go because, naturally, we want relief from our pain.

So we try to push the pain away. But healing happens through embrace, not exile.

Awareness enables us to make the unconscious... conscious. Liberation happens when we see what's holding us back—not to shame it or fight it, but to hear its message. With that information, we can make healthier choices.

The question, "What do you want to let go of?" *immediately* lets more Light into your life.

So much healing comes from simply being *curious* about our reactivity. Curiosity is medicine.

What follows isn't a fix-it list. It's a recognition guide, exploring the top five patterns many of us experience and want to release. Think of them as road signs rather than diagnoses.

What underlies all these patterns is the desire to rid ourselves of fear. Fear has many faces: fear of rejection and isolation, fear for safety and security, fear of loss or disconnection, and fear of further pain and fear.

But fear doesn't respond well to force. It does better with compassion. And companionship.

When we realize that we're not alone in our fears of the future, the unknown, or failure, we feel more connected to humanity and become so much more accepting of what's been stirring within.

We're not trying to kick these patterns to the curb. No, darling, that rejection reflex is what's been causing us problems. **The healing move is integration—blessing it.**

We get curious, and we show compassion. Because what we banish always comes back, wanting to belong. And what we bless transforms into Wisdom.

The Top 5 Patterns People Want To Let Go Of

You might see yourself in all of these or feel called to one in particular. Trust what resonates. Bless it all.

1. We want to let go of striving to be "worthy."

- Still vying to prove your "worth" despite all your inner work
- Feeling like accomplishments, material possessions, or conformity qualify you for respect and belonging
- Living like your value comes from being productive and having the future mapped out
- Feeling guilty when you rest because you think that if you rest, it will all fall apart

What to bless & release: The unhealed part of you that feels like it needs to prove it's worthy of love.

As the fears present themselves, work with them one at a time in your blessing practice. They will likely be attached to relationship and work dynamics, and anxiety that surfaces about the future. Name the fear, and bring it into your heart for the energy work.

Striving to be worthy is exhausting, darling. And harsh self-judgment is a false motivator. Your value as a human being does not come from your output. Use that energy to make choices based on Joy.

2. We want to let go of trying to control outcomes and other people.

- Managing other people's emotions and reactions because you're the responsible one
- Micromanaging details and overplanning for potential outcomes that you instinctively know are out of your control
- Overanalyzing the potential meaning or consequences, keeping your mind working overtime
- Being reluctant to admit that you think you need to be right, all the time

What to bless & release: The unhealed part of you that feels like control ensures its survival.

What's under the fear that needs to be shown some compassion? Work specifically with those emotions. Is it the fear of abandonment, of loneliness, of falling apart? The fear of what might happen if you let go of expectations or raise your expectations? The resentment and the guilt of resentment?

The relentless pursuit of control suffocates our creative agency. It blocks synchronicities from happening. The only thing you need to control is your intention—your *focused positive intention.*

3. We want to let go of replaying past pain and guilt.

- Replaying "if only" scenarios about how it could have gone differently
- Feeling like you can't move on until you get closure—mutual agreement, an apology, or justice
- Feeling like you can't move on without being expressly forgiven
- Harbouring resentment, guilt, or regrets—even though you know this creates obstacles to happiness and opportunities

What to bless & release: The unhealed parts of you that are currently experiencing disappointment, grief, and resentment.

How are those emotions showing up in your everyday life? Today's feelings are surely reflections of the past, but it's more manageable to bless what's surfacing in your daily life. That energy work will begin to soften the emotions that go back years.

The Higher Mind works forward and backward in time. If we can meet what's happening today with Acceptance and Compassion, then we start to accept and have compassion for past hurts and longings. It's not magical thinking. Blessing work gives you insight and Wisdom, which help you to move forward.

About closure... Closure doesn't require mutual agreement or buy-in from the other people involved. If we waited for everyone to see things our way before we moved forward, we'd *never* move forward.

Closure is an inside job.

Healing past hurts is Super Blesser work. It's a big deal; it's what occupies and befuddles most of us.

We create more pain in our lives when we operate in "wounded" mode. What we focus on expands. When we focus on pain, we receive more pain.

Focus your mind upward—on your Light and its qualities of clarity and luminosity. Blessing work is the fastest way to realize your own Divine Power. And the easiest way to align with the Truth that will set you free.

4. We want to let go of allowing fear to steer.

- Being hypervigilant and scanning for problems
- Habitually bracing for impact
- Ruminating and replaying *what-ifs?* and unwanted future scenarios
- Using worrying as a form of preparation
- Worrying about things you know you can't control and feeling pressure to immediately improve the things within your control
- Feeling overwhelmingly anxious about the state of the world more often than not

What to bless & release: The unhealed part of you that's scared of... *fill in the blank.*

Rejection. Abandonment. Loss of people, money, status. Some of our fears are easily traced to early life experiences. Others seem to be carried in from other incarnations. Some fears feel like they're not even ours, but we carry them nonetheless. We obsess about some fears and wonder why they materialize in our lives.

Sometimes, trying to figure out where our fears originate only distracts us from our healing. The origin does not matter as much as *how we meet our fears in real time*—meet them with total and utter Compassion.

5. We want to let go of frustrating relationship dynamics.

- Getting defensive or argumentative when feeling fear, confusion, or disappointment (the "fight" default stress reaction)
- Leaving or avoiding when feeling fear, confusion, or disappointment (the "flight" default stress reaction)
- Shutting down when feeling fear, confusion, or disappointment (the "freeze" default stress reaction)
- Fawning to maintain emotional safety or get acceptance
- Seeking validation from people who aren't as committed to the relationship
- Trying to fix others in an attempt to get needs met
- Over compromising for extended periods to avoid confrontation or pain

- Being highly reactive to parents' or other people's opinions and behaviour
- Saying "yes" when it's not *wholehearted*—doing things you don't want to do, too often

What to bless & release: The unhealed parts of you that want to be seen, heard, and loved—the most fundamental human needs!

To be clear, the HEALED parts of us *also* have these needs, but manage them in healthier ways.

Even though the results of our "letting go" survey ranked "wanting to let go of frustrating relationship dynamics" in fifth place, I think most of the other topics are tied to relationships. We're so immersed in our human connections, in general, that relationship dynamics aren't the first pain point that comes to mind.

We want to let go of striving to be "worthy" because we measure our worth using the approval of others.

We want to let go of trying to control outcomes and other people—usually so that we can have our needs met within our relationships.

We want to let go of replaying past pain and guilt. Much of which comes from interactions and relationships with others.

We want to let go of allowing fear to steer. Our fears of rejection and failure only exist in the context of social standards... relationships.

Relationships are the primary vehicle for all of our learning and growth. Because connection is how we reveal consciousness.

Blessing is the tincture for everything we experience and desire in all forms of relationships. It's the heart work that heals what's heavy and amplifies the Light of Love.

Chapter 11

How we hold on

Before you heal someone,
ask him if he's willing to give up
the things that make him sick.
—Hippocrates

Cultural conditioning vs. natural flow

There's a parable about two monks travelling together. They come to a rushing river where a woman is unable to cross. Monks are forbidden to touch women, and the river current is strong. The elder monk, without hesitation, picks up the woman and carries her to the other shore.

The monks continue walking, and after a while, the junior monk says, "As monks, we are not supposed to touch women. How could you carry her on your shoulders?" The older monk replies, "I put her down hours ago. Why are you still carrying her?"

When I was first told this story, I was excited about the rebellious act of Love. Love wins, monk man! But the less romantic interpretation of the story is that we carry emotional burdens way longer than necessary. Peace comes from moving on. Like a river.

It's not necessarily what happened in the past that wears us down; it's holding on to it that weighs on us.

Our unmet needs are not holding us back from fulfillment; clutching to the resentment that they were unmet is. We need to let go of our habit of hanging on too tight and too long.

And then we need to let go of criticizing ourselves for it.

Here's the pattern: Hurt and disappointment happen. We don't fully process our tender or gnarly feelings about what caused the hurt or disappointment—we like to skip this step and get away from the tender and gnarly feelings ASAP. So we "faux let go."

We move on from the person or the place, but we hold on to the emotions.

We think really hard about letting go. Over and over. We fixate on the idea of being more detached. We talk *a lot* about what we say we don't want to talk about anymore.

Then we find new circumstances—jobs, friends, partners—that appear different from those we don't want in our lives anymore.

We're eager to graduate, to free ourselves from what could potentially hurt us or disappoint us. But we're still comparing our present to our past. Moved on, but still holdin' on.

Dissociation and denial aren't viable solutions. They are the brothers of anxiety.

Dramatic goodbyes only buy us time until we get triggered by the same pattern in a different relationship.

Your mother-wound flares up in the boss-girl mastermind you were so stoked to join. Your new coach talks to you like your dad did, and you go silent. You overcommit to a new project just after letting go of your old commitments.

Then you criticize yourself for attracting the same situation, not learning the lesson, and not being over it.

That, my love, is the vicious part of the cycle!

It's not repetitive behaviour and attraction cycles that do the damage. Or even the familiar negative feelings. It's how we beat ourselves up for learning what we're learning. This is the self-rejection that comes with so much self-help.

Maybe you think you need another workshop to work it out. But I doubt it. Chances are you need to be more compassionate with yourself.

What happens when we grasp?

Why do we hold on? Because we're afraid of what might happen if we let go. It's not that complex. But holding on does complicate things.

Grasping creates a repulsion effect in our energy field—an energy dam that blocks exactly what we want: our desires fulfilled.

The nature of grasping
is unnecessary suffering.

Letting go leads to Joy.

When we drop the grasping, what fills the space that was occupied by control and criticism?

You. Your true, luminous presence—less driven by validation or a need for a future forecast.

You, stronger. Better able to serve yourself and the people you want to serve.

You, lighter. Relieved of old stories and full of gratitude.

My Bless & Release Journal

Re: I decide to leave a situation that I committed to, and I feel some guilt.

> *My Higher Guidance is clear, I have to go in another direction, but I'm going to disappoint some people by changing my mind. I feel guilty and gross about the conversation I am about to have with them. I need to head into a meeting with them momentarily, so I only have a quick minute to do some Centering with it.*
>
> *Quickly, I think about the sky and how my heart is that vast. I love the sky. I see one word typed in the center of my golden heart chakra (in old typewriter font, in uppercase): GUILT.*
>
> *I breathe. Colours. Light. Breathe. The big bold GUILT word gets fuzzier, more granulated. I feel lighter. I feel more loving towards myself. I can see that I'm making the right choice. I see the guilt turn into a tiny note tucked into the back corner of my heart.*
>
> *I feel clear-minded and loving. We have a great conversation about the change in plans.*

4 Things to Know About Resistance

> *Resistance to unwanted circumstances has the power to keep those circumstances alive and well for a very long time.*
> —Pema Chödrön, *When Things Fall Apart*

Healthy resistance is how we deny the darkness its power. It's an expression of Right Action. It's heart centered. It applies steady pressure towards progress.

The difference between healthy and unhealthy resistance is the difference between being grounded and being entrenched.

Unhealthy resistance says: *This can't be happening. If only I were different. If only they were different. Why me? Not again. I'm failing at manifesting. I've lost faith. I can't trust my instincts.*

Unhealthy resistance is a cocktail of denial and despair with a side of self-pity. Here's how it hurts us.

1. Resistance to what's happening is how we stay dissatisfied.

When we're so focused on *not wanting what we've got*, it gets harder to attract what we do want.

2. The more we resist our current situation, the longer we'll stay in the dynamic, and the harder it will feel.

Whether it's work, family, friendships, or romantic relationships, what we're chronically complaining about keeps getting heavier to carry, and builds more tension.

3. When we resist what's happening, we can't get to the root of our suffering.

We can't see beyond our disappointment to what's really causing it. Resistance blocks insight and the relief that comes with insight.

4. Resistance to what's happening in our lives can be a form of hostility towards ourselves.

Why's that? Because resistance—refusal, complaint, denial—means that we don't trust what we've created, what the Divine is giving us, or our capacity to shift it.

If we embrace and move into Acceptance, we see that we have the resources to either improve our situation or to pivot.

Better or *bye!*

Chapter 12

4 ways we push away what we most want

1. Excessive force

Receptivity empowers you. Forcefulness depletes you.

Newton's third law of motion says that: **for every action, there is an equal and opposite reaction.** It means that pushing on an object causes that object to push back against you.

This is why ultimatums rarely work.

This is why choosing is always better than chasing.

Forcing people to make decisions or to get on board with our ideas...

Forcing business deals to close, or projects to launch...

Forcing investments of time, money, or energy to pay off sooner...

All that pushing creates *pushback*.

Forcefulness isn't just loud and overt; it can be very subtle. A lion or a mosquito. It doesn't matter how it looks; it functions the same way.

Using force as a way of life is working harder, not smarter. And it will harden you.

When we're pushing against our reality, including other people or plans, all the time, we're in a state of repulsion. We're increasing the repelling *vibration* in our field—and the likelihood of pushback.

Too often, we hyperfocus on what we *don't* want and call that goal setting. When forcefulness dominates our energy field for long periods, it creates a repulsion force field. Our desires ricochet off us.

So the simple question becomes:

What* energy *are you exerting?

Force or flow?

Fear or faith?

Force will attract pushback, while flow will magnetize momentum.

. . .

Are there things in life to push for? Of course! Success requires vision *and* exertion. Enthusiasm, however, is a very different frequency than forcefulness. It's inspired from within, from a sense of fullness, whereas force and pushiness usually come from fear, a sense of lack, or resentment.

Let's use a dating example. Say you want to find a life partner, so you decide to start dating.

Wait... quick tangent:

Manifestation is not a numbers game. It's an energy game. So going on a lot of dates doesn't necessarily increase your odds of meeting your person. Being a vibrational match for what you desire is what registers in the energy field. More on that later.

Back to dating...

You're forcing yourself to get out there and date because you feel needy and alone. What's driving your behaviour is actually the repulsion of your own desires. On top of that, maybe you feel unworthy because you haven't manifested what you want yet. Self-criticism is a powerfully destructive motivator.

On every date you're forcing yourself to go on, your energy field is signalling, "I don't want to be needy and alone, and I'm failing because I feel needy and alone."

So your experiences reflect your repulsion to needy-aloneness energy. And you attract people you don't feel connected to.

By the way, it is not ridiculous to feel needy and alone; it's part of the human experience. We just need to be compassionate with it, not repulsed by it.

Fast-forward to a more balanced you. You've been doing the Centering Practice on the daily, blessing & releasing all the time, working with your fears, lighting up your desires. Relaxation and trust have taken root—through consistent Compassion and visioning. Even though you still feel needy and alone some days, you're more at ease with it. Rather than being repulsed by your humanity, you're softened by it.

You've brought the pain and fear into your heart center and effectively raised the vibration of "needy and alone" to Acceptance and Love.

Now, from this sense of fullness, you decide to date, driven by pleasure instead of pain. You're full of beautiful possibilities. And like attracts like, so... swipe right, babe.

Once you stop forcing what you want to happen, you're halfway to getting it!

2. Retelling old stories

Some people talk mostly about their past and wonder why their present isn't what they want it to be.

When we keep talking about what we want to let go of, our words keep us holding on.

We water down the truth for fear of what it could lead to.

We break our word—self-sabotage that blocks real progress.

We say negative things to ourselves to keep our stress levels high—because the familiar feels strangely more comforting than the unknown.

This may be an overgeneralization (but probably not): I put entrepreneurs in two broad camps—ones who are great at letting go and those who don't know they're stuck in the past. Guess who tends to be more successful?

When someone comes to me for a strategy session, I'll ask, "So what's the big vision? What would light you up?" If they look in the rearview mirror and say, "I was really happy when I was at the agency years ago... I loved it when...," I'll try to coax them into the present. "Okay, so what are you excited about *now*?" And back they go, "Well, what I used to do was..."

I breathe into my impatient entrepreneurial heart.

"K, let's hit pause on the past. Dream with me," I'll say. "*Moving on*, what would 'ideal' look like?"

And then if they tell me why a project never launched, all I can offer is, "Do 21 days of *The Centering Practice,* and DM me."

Success or failure is often about the stories we tell. We can over-identify with our past, or we can identify with our fulfilled future self.

Every time we retell a painful story, we re-activate that dynamic. It's like watering the weeds in your energy field. "The thing that happened" slips in and distracts us from possibility thinking.

I'm not suggesting that we should never talk about our pasts again (though that's not an entirely bad idea). The ego loves a good replay and kvetch. But what if we only speak about our struggles with the intention of healing more deeply, or to help someone with our story?

Or maybe we could let the old story rest—so that we can rise.

3. Feeling guilty about feeling guilty

Guilt is such a complex emotion, but it's how the ego keeps us from moving on.

First, we have to make a distinction: there's our conscience, or moral compass, and then there's guilt.

Conscience is your Soul nudging you to come back to balance. It says, "Did it feel good to do what you did? I don't think it felt good. How about we clean that up so we feel more aligned?" Consciousness is the keeper of karma. It calls us forward.

Guilt pulls us back. It's critical and slightly paranoid, and it says that it's all our fault.

Conscience will guide us to take Right Action. In the Buddhist tradition, Right Action is ethical and intentional conduct, choosing to act in ways that do not cause harm and, ideally, that bring benefit.

We have to work with both our shadow guilt and our conscious guilt. It all belongs. When you bring the guilt into your heart center, it will dissolve into empathy for yourself and others.

4. Complaining, blaming, & shaming

> *Blame is the world's greatest excuse. It enables us to remain limited and small without feeling guilty. But there is a cost—the loss of our freedom.*
>
> —David Hawkins, *Letting Go: The Pathway of Surrender*

Complaints escalate into blame. And blaming always leads to shame.

A team member of mine quit and wrote me a 2-page letter telling me how much I sucked. The reason that was shocking wasn't the 17 bullet points listing my flaws. It was because just 2 weeks earlier, they'd sent me flowers and said they wanted to work with me until they retired, *go all the way, mama!* I was surprised to learn I apparently sucked now.

Sometimes, there's no bless. It's just *Whack! I'm outta here!* That can do some damage. If we're not comfortable feeling a range of emotions, then big feelings can seem threatening. And it can be hard to be graceful when we're scared. So we might use negative reasoning—complaining, blaming, shaming—to armour up.

And sometimes we end up blaming ourselves. Either way, blame is a low-vibration energy that creates a lot of congestion and confusion.

Go time

When a dream has died, we don't need to denigrate the dream. "I was a fool to chase that... It was never going to work..." Nah. You were living. And now it's time to dream a new dream.

We can let go simply because it's time. Our inner guidance sends us a memo that we're ready for a change. And it might be sad, and there will likely be some grief, but it's the natural order of things. No one has to suck. It's just... time.

Your past is not a graveyard of unmanifested dreams. Let it rest in your heart so that your Life Force can be freed up to create the future. And babe, your past does not define your future. Not even close.

Don't try to outrun the impact of all those yesterdays—that's how we come undone, drained of hope. We need you well-resourced and facing forward.

Bless everything before today. All of it.

And you know what happens when you extend appreciation to your past? You get access to your complete catalogue of purpose and power—your full potential—all complements of your past.

Chapter 13

Conscious relating is conscious creating

Relationship reminders

- Every relationship is a divine assignment. Parents, loves of our lives, teachers, dogs, customer service reps. *Every single one.*
- Every interaction—even with ourselves—is put on our path so we can learn to love more.
- Pain in any form is a cry for love.
- All conflict is a call for unity.
- Whomever is right in front of us is our spiritual practice.
- Healing ourselves is an act of love for the world.

"Every relationship is a divine assignment" is a poetic way of saying: we trigger each other into wholeness. A former partner and I were so triggered once that we argued over who was more triggerable.

Relationship goals.

We activate each other's wounds so that we can become our own healers.

Once you start working on the energetic level—directly with your heart—old identity narratives loosen up. Meaning, how you see yourself and the other person begins to shift, usually towards Compassion and understanding.

A woman in our Centered Community was having a hard time with her adult daughter. She was really debating the right thing to do. "I don't know if I should text my kid or call her, or would that be more triggering? Maybe I should pay for the vacation, but just for her, but that could upset her husband, and then she'd be mad at me, and they wouldn't come for holidays. I've tried everything."

"Have you tried working with the energy of this?" I asked. Pause. "Like, just work with your feelings. Sit in your backyard and bring her into your heart. Take it out of strategy mode and pour some light on the frustration. THEN decide if you're going to text or call her." Mama Blesser reported back that their next visit was the easiest in a long time.

It's all divine timing.

Who's being vilified and demonized?
Bless them.

Who's caused you hurt?
Bless them.

Who continues to treat you poorly?
Bless them.

Energy work in relationships is not a quick fix (though I have seen some amazing revelations and mindset shifts). But over time, you'll notice that the volume and viciousness of your own reactivity decrease.

Then, when you get irritated or scared, you *consciously decide to love your way through it.*

And that's what it's all about!

Conscious relating is conscious creating.

The frustrating as f*ck circular conversations, the huffing and puffing, eye rolling, crying in the shower, avoiding, fawning, and refusing but then giving in... those are all opportunities to *decide to love your way through it.* Instead of fighting, flighting, freezing, or fawning your way around it.

HOW will you love your way through it? You will do the energy work that changes your perspectives and behaviours.

You will breathe into your heart, bring in the frustration, and do some light work with it. You will exhale.

Bless it, instead of chastising it.

Integration, not exile.

It's not you, it's me (and my energy)

Emotional intimacy is one of our greatest strengths. It's hard work at times, but we can do hard work *gently.* That approach changes everything. A soft gaze on raw feelings, a gentle touch on the heavy topics. Rainbow-coloured light on your triggers.

Blessing & releasing can be arduous. Gentle rhythmic breathing? That'll crack you open. Those shimmering light frequencies can feel like a tsunami. On a Sunday, The Centering Practice can get you high on life. On a Monday, it can make you sob in the kitchen because grief has shown up for some attention.

When you want to shut down, choose to breathe in the desire to shut down. When you want to blame, breathe in the desire to blame. You don't judge your stress response. And don't skip ahead to imagining outcomes. Stay with what's happening in the moment so that your emotional discomfort doesn't build into blame—of yourself or others.

Blaming others can be a way of bypassing how we're really feeling. Saying "You're late again" to your late-again partner is a statement of fact. Blaming shows up in the tone. And the blame is likely a cover-up for feeling disrespected.

They're late. Again. You're resentful. Your first job is to get truthful about how you feel, not what you think of their behaviour. Take the attention off them. Start with you.

Bless & release. Bring it into your heart, think a positive thought about anything at all, then give your resentment some light frequencies.

Remember: Blessing is not condoning or bypassing. It's presence and power!

The love that you give your emotions helps your mind and body—your nervous system—to calm down. The stories get less chatty. The mind cools.

And then you can think about what you want to do with your late-again partner. Share how you really feel, laugh it off, or come up with a new deal.

Build all relationships on your commitment to truth

Blessing is a form of forgiving. You forgive yourself. You forgive others. You start forgiving the micro-moments (and so much of our relationships happen in micro-moments).

Forgiving is not acquiescing. It gives you the confidence to live in Truth. Then you can make the best moves for your growth: to let go of the pattern but keep the person, or to release the relationship container altogether.

Your focus will be less on what anyone did or could have done to make things better, and more on who you are today and who you want to become.

Breathe steady with your fluctuating emotions. Get very, very soft around your rage—and even softer with the shame of your rage. Hold your exhaustion like it's an egg… incubating with beautiful potential in your heart chakra.

Accept this truth: YOU are the healer.

Soul contracts under review

> *Beware of the temptation to perceive yourself unfairly treated.*
> *—A Course in Miracles*

When we're afraid or hurt, the Lower Mind looks around for whose fault it is.

Our shadow self builds the case for why we're right and should take space or withhold love. Or why we're justified for leaving. We turn our relationships into trials and negotiations. Sometimes, literally.

Our hurt is very real to each of us. And we can be totally right, take some space, even leave *without making anyone else responsible for our feelings.*

That might seem like a tall order, but let me give you some meta perspective (we'll get into this more deeply soon). Most of our current feelings are rooted in past experiences. They hang out in our unconscious self. Some of those feelings aren't even related to this lifetime. We've incarnated to transmute those feelings into insight so that we can better embody Divine Love.

From our ego's point of view, relationship challenges—and endings—are the fault of the other person: *They don't take accountability. They're dishonest. They don't care enough. They didn't share enough.*

But it's never entirely about the "other." It's about our energy field and the beliefs we've got to release. Yes, they may not have been accountable, or maybe they were dishonest… Not. Very. Mindful. But something in our field is magnetizing the experience and attaching it to us.

This does not mean that we're responsible for anybody else's behaviour or feelings, or that we should stick around for sh*tty treatment. But no matter which path we travel, or who we choose to do life with, we can be certain that the unconscious will stir up exactly what needs to be seen, heard, and held by us.

Our wounds have nothing to do with the other. This can be a tough realization. We are either responding proactively to our pain points and learning to hold ourselves with grace, or we're responding reactively and causing ourselves more pain. We bless, or we resist.

We incarnate whole and complete. As we go through life, we are conditioned to various beliefs, particularly the belief that we're broken and need to be "fixed." We don't. In fact, it makes no sense given that we're here to realize our innate perfection—our True Nature. If we are made in the image of the Creator, what's to be fixed?

The next obvious question, then, is: Why do we treat each other so poorly? War, war, and more war? The answer is, again, because we are conditioned to various beliefs, particularly the belief that we're broken and need to be "fixed." All madness, in its varying degrees, comes from the illusion that we're unworthy and separate from the Source. We're all just acting out until we realize the Truth.

This is our biggest assignment. Rediscovering the divine fact that we're whole, complete, and fully intact exactly as we are. Acceptance.

From a metaphysical perspective, relationship challenges and endings are the natural order of life. They are karmic. The purpose is always to learn to love our way through it. This is the toughest assignment in Earth school.

To be graceful when you're feeling ground down. To choose inner knowing and dignity over blame.

On the surface, there are reasons that the relationship isn't working—resentments, restrictions, and weaknesses. But when relationships end, it's because our Soul contract is up. The learning is complete. Planetary alignments have danced it out.

Whether it's with a boss, a partner, or a long-time friend—whether we grew apart or betrayal burned the bridge—we end relationships when we don't want the heavy energies in our field anymore. Play the blame game, though, and we will carry that vibration with us. We don't have to take responsibility for anybody else's actions. We can't. Ever. But we can be radically responsible for what we came to learn.

Blessing dissolves the bonds of karma and lets us leave with a clean conscience.

That's the curriculum for heart centered life.

My Bless & Release Journal

> *I was sitting at my desk crying as I Googled, "How to overcome heroin addiction." Except, I've never tried heroin. I don't even drink coffee.*
>
> *I was trying to let go of divorce pain. My mind-looping felt addictive, and I wondered if recovery methods were transferable.*
>
> *I felt bound and brittle. I knew that I had to become the antidote to that—open and fluid. So I did the most radical thing I could think of: a 21-day Centering Practice for my former husband. No skipping days. All in.*

Prior, I'd been trying to keep him off my doorstep. But now I was going to hold him in the cave of my heart with unconditional Love and recall the best parts of our relationship. It was worth a shot.

It was really hard.

And then it was awesome.

On day 1, I just sobbed through all the light streaming. The next day, I cried for his pain. Then the next day, I cried for our son. Then one morning, as I was letting the grief relax in my heart, I remembered why I fell in love with him. I saw resentment hiding behind my blame. I saw the perfection in all of it. I saw how vast my heart is—it's so big!

Soon enough, I was pouring cherishing energy all over him. Waves of Love. It was so easy. I started looking forward to my daily bless session.

I considered putting his new girlfriend in the light bubble, but like, let's not get carried away. When the 21 days were up, I'd done what I needed to. I transmuted a hella heap of pain. And that was my closure.

Years have gone by since then, and I still draw on that cherishing energy... and it softens me. Which is an upgrade to being a brittle cow about things.

Some romantic endings are abrupt. Some involve a slow crawl of counselling, waffling, and reconciliation booty calls all the way to the finish line. Or so I'm told.

Resentment, hostility, vengefulness, spite. Who needs it? Not you. Not them. Not anyone around you. Doing the light work with those heavy emotions is how we get strong and move on.

You’re not the weather.
You’re the sky.

Chapter 14

The magnetism of thoughts… and feelings

Let thoughts and feelings have their home in you, but don't make your home in them.
—Rupert Spira, *The Ashes of Love*

Where do feelings come from?

Most pain comes from unprocessed thoughts and feelings.

Feelings happen first because they're biochemical. Emotions are more psychological. Emotions are what your mind thinks about your feelings. For the purposes of this conversation, we can use thoughts, emotions, and feelings interchangeably—all of them need to be integrated into our hearts to come into balance.

It's helpful to understand that feelings come from the subconscious self. They hang out in the shadow territories.

All emotions carry a message for us. Every single feeling arises to be experienced and integrated into our hearts.

The stronger the negative feeling, the closer it is to an unhealed wound.

Even though emotions can swing the pendulum between pleasure and pain, they aren't "bad" or base. What's problematic is when we over-identify with our emotions and get pulled off center into highs and lows.

The Buddha taught, "All suffering comes from identification." When you identify as sad, mad, angry, or glad, you're like a leaf in a wind of emotional flurries.

You're not the weather. You're the sky. Spacious awareness. Infinite capacity.

Critical thinking without the criticism

> *When we don't feel things, they don't touch us deeply enough to create real change.*
> —Thomas Hübl, *Healing Collective Trauma*

When I was in my 20s, I'd bus to the Seattle Buddhist Center on Tuesday nights for Vipassana meditation. I'd leave my Doc Martens at the door, get into lotus position, and follow the instructions to watch my in-breath and out-breath. Whenever a thought crossed my mind, I was to simply name it as "thinking."

So my inner dialogue sounded like this: *thinking, thinking, thinking, more thinking... I'm still f*cking thinking.*

After a few weeks, the very sweet instructor asked me how I was doing. "Well... my mind feels emptier," I said. "But so does my heart."

She was sympathetic, and she encouraged me to stick with it. But I bailed.

I could not figure out how watching my breath would make me a better person or help me attract my soul mate. *Enough of the mind stuff, I want the heart stuff! I'm a lover, not a stoic!* So I started studying *A Course in Miracles*. It was the heart-centered cosmology that suited me best back then.

Over time, my cravings became even more evident. I wanted the Light! I wanted to be saturated with luminosity. I wanted a vivacious kind of devotion. This is why blessing protocols and light frequencies are at the center of my life now.

What I didn't understand back then was that noticing my thinking wasn't meant to be a judgment of my thinking. Noticing, good. Judging, not as good. That was a Beginner Buddhist fail. I thought that the goal was to get rid of my thoughts—and to critique them before I booted them.

I thought the Buddhist path to enlightenment was very, very stern. Which was probably a hangover from Catholic guilt. Which I was trying to positively think my way out of. You can see why I bailed.

We can only heal what we honour.

What I wish I had known in my early Buddhist adventuring was that the inhale does the blessing, the exhale does the releasing—and it's *all* in my energy field.

The practice of allowing
our thoughts
to come and go
without judgment
is a great act of love.

Name your feelings

Unacknowledged feelings become emotional clutter. They'll keep trying to get our attention with mind looping, anxiety, neuroses, and dread. When a painful part of our history and negative emotions are pushed aside, they get stronger and more painful. In psychology, it's called *amplification*. In real life, it's called *I should have dealt with my stuff a while ago because now it's comin' for me.*

Neuroscience proves that identifying what we're feeling can significantly reduce the intensity. Putting feelings into words reduces activity in the amygdala—the part of the brain that processes emotions. Naming feelings helps the brain shift from reactivity to regulation, from overwhelm to awareness. In psychology, this is called *affect labelling.* In real life, it's called *getting real.*

Acknowledge your feelings so they can move through you. That's all they want. To be seen in micro acts of consciousness.

We don't have to journal about them, though we could. We don't have to create a story around why we feel rejected and who rejected us, and their trauma and our re-trauma. That's narrative processing gone wrong; it just re-energizes the negative feelings.

(And not all painful emotions are traumatizing. Pain can just be pain. Labelling every painful occurrence as "trauma" is like calling every traffic light a roadblock.)

Acknowledging feelings and sensations can be a way of processing them lightly. We don't have to process everything deeply to make progress. It can be like this:

Huh, I felt this flare of anger when they said that. Interesting. That's it. *Hi, anger. I see you.* Carrying on.

Sometimes, it's very worthwhile to dissect the *where-what-why* of an emotional reaction. I spent years in therapy doing just that. For sure, the standout emotions are worthwhile blessings—which have saved me thousands on therapy.

Acknowledging your feelings is like blowing clouds away. You create more mental clarity.

Our thoughts become our chemistry

Different thoughts and images in our mind release different concentrations of chemicals in our brains that either fuel or deplete us.

Our brain behaves like a chemist, converting thoughts, perceptions, and ideas into chemical signals (dopamine, cortisol, oxytocin, etc.) that are released into the bloodstream. Loving, positive thoughts create nourishing chemistry. Unconscious fears and phobias trigger stress chemistry that wears us down.

My Bless & Release Journal

Re: Scared about the future outcome.

I hadn't been wanting to admit that I was feeling scared about the future of a project I'd been working on. I was stiff-upper-lipping it. I finally had to admit at the end of a long day that, yep, I was a bit freaked out.

I did a little Centering Practice in the bathtub. I brought in the freaked-out feeling, and I immediately felt so much more relaxed. I felt less silly for being freaked out. I could see that doubt doesn't predict failure; I can just let it pass through.

With that cleared up, I could see where the glitch in my project had occurred and how to solve it. The solution was hiding behind the fear gremlin. If I'd sucked it up and pushed away the fear, I wouldn't have seen the solution.

Everybody has their feelings

Feelings hang out in the subconscious self—the basement of the psyche. The subconscious self keeps tugging to say, "Hey… there's this emotion down here that needs some light."

Surprise meltdowns can happen to the wisest of us. If I've learned anything from being in the wellness community most of my life, it's that *no one* is immune to being blindsided by their shadow. We all meet God when we beg for relief.

I know of a venerated monk who had anxiety attacks when he left the monastery. And a devout theologian whose romantic fixation broke his faith and sank him into deep depression. One of my favourite meditation teachers, a true master, went on anti-anxiety meds to help manage PTSD from years of chronic physical pain.

The path to Higher Consciousness always travels through the lower realms of the unconscious. The holy is in our humanity.

Meeting our pain with Loving Kindness is what it actually means to be enlightened.

That's it.

Nondualism? It's nice if you can get it. Feeling one with the cosmos? Excellent.

But the hallmark of illumination is saying this one phrase to your dark side, over and over again: "I hear you, and I've got you."

I used to think that it was better to find my pain before it found me. I was always poking at my wounds with yet another therapist or 3-day intensive workshop. But the subconscious gremlins are unpredictable; they do not operate on linear time. Stuff comes up when it needs to come up. We can't control the trigger sources. We can, however, become really agile at handling what happens when we're inevitably triggered.

To make friends with our pain, we need to ask its name. *Shameful, insecure, unattractive, needy, abandoned, furious, dirty, sad, hella uncontrollable but freakishly controlling, confused.*

It can be awkward. I'm sometimes shocked by the replies from my inner shadow. I call her "Shadow D." I check in with her in the morning and every night when I'm in bed. It's simple. I put my right hand on my belly and my left hand on my heart, and I inquire, *How you feeling? What do you need from me? How can I help you come into balance?*

Sometimes she'll say, *I hope we walk in the woods today.* Or, *More yoga makes me happy.* Other days, she might scream, *I'm so f*cking afraid!*

And I think, *Is this voice really a part of me, or is this some rando radio wave I'm picking up? I'm brave. I've got my sh*t together. How could I have an unhinged, terrified part of me that's yelling at me at 6am?*

But I've learned that it is indeed my unconscious self, and sometimes she's terrified, and it's my job—it's my honour, actually—to respond lovingly.

I hear you, and I've got you.

Facing our feelings

> *Let everything happen to you: beauty and terror. Just keep going. No feeling is final.*
> —Rainer Maria Rilke, *Go to the Limits of Your Longing*

As a society, we're just getting started with emotional literacy. As Carl Jung put it, "People will do anything, no matter how absurd, in order to avoid facing their own souls." Mostly, we ignore our wild depths.

Overachieving is a great distraction from feeling unworthy. So, we overwork. A lot. We create new distractions from the old distractions. A romance, a remodelling project, a new goal to crush immediately after slaying the last goal in our life-hacking plan.

The pain gremlins in the basement of our psyche pound harder on the ceiling... *I still don't feel heard. You're moving too fast to listen. Where am I on your calendar?* And our shadow self starts to yank on our nervous system.

Then the hormones that help us regulate stress get sluggish. The emotions get even more intense. We might shut down on the sofa for days. Or we have a panic attack on a Zoom call. We scroll and scroll and... scroll. *It can get hard to tell the difference between priorities and polarities.*

This is a form of self-preservation.

Whatever we've buried in our emotional backyard, we put there so we could get on with things. At the time of the hurtful or traumatic event, it made perfect sense to tamp down shame, rage, or the pain of rejection. It was an excellent survival strategy. We were younger and less resourced, and we needed to stay intact while we kept moving.

But now we're ready to be whole—spiritually mature adults. Conscious creators.

Imagine this: Instead of feeling like a loser because you're worrying about something, you breathe into your heart. You engage with the worried, difficult feelings. You say to your inner Worry Willa, "I hear you. You're telling me something. You can sit in my heart, and I'll breathe. When you show up, it helps me to remember my faith, so thank you."

Every emotion can benefit us if we get curious about it.

When we bless our worries with loving attention, we see *their* value, and *they* relax.

What would it be like to show some respect to your shame? That's a big one. Shame-y energy likes to hide in dark corners, hoping it never gets talked about. But it's like that nerdy Goth girl who wants to come out into the sun and socialize. What if you gave her back some dignity?

"Hey... Shame Ella, I see you. I get why you feel the way you do—it's understandable. So understandable. Listen, you're welcome to stay in my heart while I get some work done. Stay and relax, and I'm going to go on living, making things I'm proud of."

Shame is sacred. Your heart is safe.

All feelings calm down when they're welcomed in. Same with most people.

Making negative feelings positive is not what it's about. It's about Acceptance. Once we accept a feeling, it evolves; it shifts. We don't ask a crying friend not to cry. We don't ask our doubt to turn into faith or our sadness to get happy. We meet it where it's at.

Make space for shame, and you can use the freed-up energy to carry on. The shame-y shamed part of you exhales and leans back.

Bless your anxiety and go for a walk.

You know that part of you that's so pissed off it won't shut up? Bless it with some attention, and then you can pivot towards peace.

This is key: We're not blessing our heavy emotions to shut them up, so we can think more about why we're upset. No, no, darling. This is bless & *release*, not bless & re-hash.

Bless and get on with your day, your moment, and your work in the world.

Love neutralizes emotions—this is a good thing

> *Our feelings are only ever pleasant or unpleasant, and never right or wrong.*
> *This is something Buddhist psychology strongly emphasizes...*
> *You need not be ashamed of any feeling you experience. You feel what you feel.*
> *Simply accepting this is in itself a profound act of self-compassion.*
> —Bodhipaksa

Here's the healing move: curiosity over judgment.

Every single time you observe your emotions, thoughts, or behaviour... hold the judgment, and look with curiosity.

This is the work of self-agency. Being the leader of your own life experience. If you're not leading it, who is?

Think of yourself as the queen of hearts. Or a majestic king. Think: *I am the powerful and benevolent ruler of my life.* Anytime anything crosses your desk, or wants your attention, or stands before you, ask, *Who do we have here?* Inquire with composure, with a dignified demeanour.

Because it's a joy to lead with Love.

Regard all experiences and emotions that enter your kingdom with respect. *With curiosity. With compassion.* These are very potent types of energy. Curiosity and compassion neutralize emotional swings and take the charge out of reactions to challenges.

Am I saying you should say respectful things to your rage or the anxiety that's been kicking your ass? I think it's worth a try. It's what your nervous system is hoping for.

Bless your thoughts

I've tried emptying my mind of thoughts. Didn't work. I still thought about not having thoughts. That's the thing with the mind: it's always thinking about itself. Trying to wrestle with thoughts that we don't want can perpetuate more thinking that we *do not* want. It's exasperating.

We exist, we think, we feel. But we tend to overthink, get consumed by feelings, and forget that we are pure energy in constant motion.

Thoughts and emotions intertwine. One influences the other. Thoughts can stir up feelings; feelings can direct thoughts. It really doesn't matter which comes first.

You can have a peaceful relationship with a noisy mind. Peace doesn't come from trying to tame the Lower Mind. It comes from befriending it.

This is why blessing happens in the heart space—in our Higher Consciousness.

What we're *really* "letting go of" is lower-vibration thinking.

By "letting go," we mean integrating—and therefore transforming—our denser frequency thoughts into higher, more refined vibrations. The Higher Mind giving guidance to the Lower Mind.

By "letting go," we mean offering up and surrendering our ideas about ourselves, people, places, and experiences.

By "letting go," we mean detaching, liberating, and emancipating.

The heart creates safety for the egoic mind to unhook and release what it's been grasping.

Which creates deep freedom. *Which is life-changing.*

> ## 2 life-changing questions:
>
> - What's the energy of the thoughts I'm thinking?
> - How am I treating my feelings? With rejection or compassion?

You get to choose the thoughts and beliefs you want to focus on, nurture, and live by. They could come from anywhere. The Bible. The Talmud. Your daily meditation. What your sister told you. The love you've been shown so many times. The dream you had. The oracle. The medicine. The algorithm that's feeding you specific "rights" and "wrongs." Your family (also likely feeding you specific "rights" and "wrongs"). Your genes. Your genius.

We can select the thoughts we want to amplify. If we don't want to think about something, we can simply *think about something else.*

My Bless & Release Journal

Re: Fear of rejection.

I'm lying on the living room floor, thinking about an upcoming trip, and a totally irrational fear enters my mind. It's bizarre and makes no sense. But I don't want the fear to take hold and become magnetic, so I decide to work with it.

It's showing me that I have an underlying fear about being rejected by someone in my life—I'm surprised by this. But I soften to it. I breathe into my heart. I think about how much I love slow mornings. I light up my heart, and I bring in the fear and stir in colour frequencies. It dissolves. I feel optimistic.

Chapter 15

The power of gentle

Cutting cords

In quantum mechanics, entanglement is the phenomenon that happens when two particles become connected in such a way that "the state of one instantly influences the other, no matter the distance between them." Two particles seem to instantly influence one other, even if they are separated by billions of light-years.

It's also a beautiful metaphor for our human bonds.

Energetically, we become entangled with others through love, trauma, and shared experience. These connections aren't inherently bad, but the way we try to sever them can either create more turbulence... or healing.

The concept of "cutting energy cords" with people and places—in which we send all that energy back to where it came from, and cut-cut-cut those cords! Well... that practice can be a powerful remedy for imbalances and to protect ourselves. *But mostly... no.*

> **You can't let go of something that you're aggressively trying to let go of.**

There may be times when you need to go full sorcerer—invoke your guardians, and with unwavering fierceness, cut the energetic ties to whatever has been menacing you. There are such initiations. But *even then*, spiritual warriors do not go into combat in a blind rage.

The darkness loves a good fight. Surprise it with composure and neutrality. Approach your cord-cutting as the duty of Right Action. We sever ties for the good of all—including whoever and whatever we are severing ties with.

For the majority of our angsty entanglements, the aggressive act of cutting cords can make a mess of things. Blessing & releasing makes for a clean exit.

Using your power for good

When you start working with heart energy, and raising your own frequency, you become more insightful. You increase your capacity to conduct Light. And become more adept at seeing your own shadow and Lower Mind choices. And you're going to be able to see it more clearly in others.

This is where we need to stay mindful of our power.

Insightfulness can turn into righteousness, a false sense of strength. Our genuine ability to see more clearly can, ironically, create a distorted sense of self. Superiority. New Age arrogance.

It happens to the best of us.

We get in touch with our pain, we master some breathwork or contemplation techniques, and we have some legit awareness experiences. We peel back layers in therapy, and we make connections to everything from our desires to our behaviour patterns. We heal some trauma. And so... we're not on the same wavelength as some people anymore.

Now we might start to think that *they* need to do more breathwork or therapy, or have some breakthroughs. They need to do some blessing & releasing to transmute their triggers.

But it's still us. It's always still us.

No matter what channel you're on, or constellation you come from, there's always blessing & releasing to do.

The tone of letting go

> *Darkness cannot drive out darkness: only light can do that.*
> *Hate cannot drive out hate: only love can do that.*
> —Reverend Dr. Martin Luther King, Jr.

Our tone manifests as much as our words do. You can shout goodbye and slam the door. Or you can say goodbye and bow. Same words. With hostility or namasté energy. Words create reality, and tone matters—a lot.

How we let go determines the effectiveness of the release. We want to let go without leaving a hook. *We want true completion.*

This can only happen when we practice harmlessness as a virtue. Harmlessness sounds lightweight, but it's a form of warriorship. It requires self-discipline and humility.

I have a friend who's the most gentle-natured human. He has big brown pacifist eyes. We went for a walk the day after a big political election. And, in reference to the winner, my mild-mannered friend said, "I wish someone would just kill him!" I winced. Politics is a sh*t show, but what I wanted to say is, "Honey, you don't want that murder vibe in your field... There's a better way to process this."

We say crazy, out-of-character things when we're anxious and angry. Understandable, but... it all gets registered in our energy field and subconscious. Malice is an energy hook. We can't build better lives with malice spinning out in our energy field.

We can speak our truth without the intention to cause harm.

With our words, blessings, curses, goodbyes, and hellos, we energize realities into form.

Wisdom of letting go

Every faith, spiritual paradigm, or religion teaches about the power of letting go.

> ✝ **Christianity.** *"Not my will, but Yours be done."*
> Core idea: Trust and surrender. Letting go is yielding one's will to God, trusting Divine Providence.

Islam and Sufism. *Surrender and trust in God's unfolding.*
Core idea: Trust and submission. Letting go is reliance on Allah, trusting His wisdom beyond human control.

Hinduism. *Act fully, release the results.*
Core idea: Detachment from outcomes. Perform actions, but release attachment to their fruits.

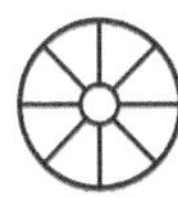

Buddhism. *Release clinging, find peace in impermanence.*
Core idea: Non-attachment. Suffering arises from clinging to impermanent things; letting go is freedom.

Judaism. *Return and renewal.*
Core idea: Sacred return. Letting go is turning back towards wholeness—releasing what separates us from our highest nature and from community.

Indigenous / First Nations. *All things renew and return.*
Core idea: Harmony with seasons. Letting go is nature's cycles: death, renewal, return.

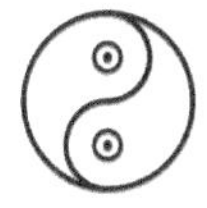

Taoism. *Flow with the way of all things.*
Core idea: Effortless flow (Wu Wei). Letting go is alignment with the Tao, to move with nature's current.

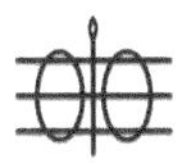

Bahá'í Faith. *Unity through detachment.*
Core idea: Progressive revelation. Letting go of rigid beliefs allows unity consciousness—all Truth is one unfolding story.

Stoicism. *Love your fate, accept what comes.*
Core idea: Acceptance. Freedom comes from focusing on what's within our control and accepting what's not.

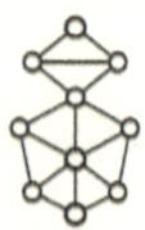

Kabbalah. *Breaking vessels to let the Light in.*
Core idea: Transformation through shattering. What breaks open makes space for divine Light. Letting go is how we heal the world.

Pagan / Celtic. *Endings are sacred beginnings.*
Core idea: Release into nature. Letting go with seasonal cycles; honouring.

Gnosticism. *Liberation through knowing.*
Core idea: Direct knowing (Gnosis). Letting go of material illusion reveals inner Divinity—you are not the body, you are eternal Light.

Hermetic / Esoteric Traditions. *As above, so below.*
Core idea: The Law of Correspondence. What we release internally transforms externally—microcosm and macrocosm mirror each other.

Metaphysical. ***Bless & release.***
Core idea: Focused positive intention circulates energy and creates wellness in all systems.

Everything is energy, and energy is always in motion.

Chapter 16

Grief

This too shall pass

I was in the middle of a breakup drama, and a sage friend said, "This too shall pass." I wanted to yell, "I don't want this to pass! If the pain goes, so does the relationship!"

This is not a healthy approach to grief, my friends.

Because I'm usually very attached to whatever/whoever is the cause of my grief, the phrase "This too shall pass" used to really trigger me.

And I didn't like its ramifications: in the highs of happiness, who wants to hear that this *too* shall pass? Not me.

Many times, I sat with the concept of impermanence and found it very, very uncomfortable. Which brings me to another phrase I don't like: "Sit with it."

As a spiritual director, I'm supposed to say, "I'm going to sit with the pain." But I don't actually want to sit with the pain. I want to do something about it. I want to move it out of my mind and body.

But facts are facts: *it will all pass,* and I need to sit with that.

Everything is energy, and energy is always in motion.

Grief is a wave of Love crashing against our illusion of separation. It's an expansion process that returns us to Source awareness. It's one of the most challenging, beautiful emotions to embrace.

Grief is the ultimate bless & release.

We heal the pain of our loss by not creating resistance to it.

But I can't think of a harder lesson. Or a more enlightening one.

Grief is rooted in the body. It's a cellular memory of what we love, loved, held, had, desired. Unattended grief creates stagnancy, and it has to be moved out of the body before it calcifies into depression or bitterness. We don't need to suffer unnecessarily to honour what we're grieving.

Grief needs movement and affection. Light heals grief. Love heals grief. Not time. We all know someone who's been holding on to the pain of a loss for years. Consciousness, not time, heals all things.

This is where the light work comes in. The active blessing of the hardest challenges. **We're not making light of our loss; *we're applying light to the pain of loss.*** We're meeting ourselves in our most vulnerable places.

Can you name what you're grieving? There are probably layers to it. It might even be collective grief you're feeling.

What's the loss, and why the sorrow? How does the sorrow affect you—your thoughts, words, actions, relationships? Are you grieving the loss of connection or the death of a dream? Is it time to bless & release hope? Because there are times to bless & release some kinds of hope.

If you've been through a grief initiation, you know that there's a strangely beautiful passage where, in the midst of your grieving, you stumble across a well of Joy. This is what happens. The grief leads you to a patch of light in the dark night. You were in the throes of wrestling with the suffering, and then suddenly you're swept away by a wave of Love for what you lost, or for just being alive. There it is—the heart of life.

Joy.

How can I feel grace in such a dark place? It will be confusing if you think about it too much. So don't think about it too much.

You can make space for grief—a weekend to spill it out, a sabbatical, a therapeutic container, deep solitude—but grief comes on her own time. We're often taken by surprise by a wave of grief, but I think that's the Divine's deliberate design. If we knew when the pain was coming, we'd probably try to avoid it or brace for impact. It's better when grief slips in.

Coping with grief in healthy ways amplifies our Radiance. Our appreciation for each other—and life itself—multiplies. We become more understanding about our light and shadow sides—and other people's light and shadow sides.

If we can be compassionate with our grief, *if* we can let our grief be at home with us, we become gentle. And wise.

Life cycles

Michael Barden was my psychotherapist on and off for over 20 years. He was a Jewish Buddhist—a Jew-Bu, as he would say—who grew up in the 1950s in Brooklyn. His office was a small room with Afghan carpets and pillows. So Michael and his people (he didn't like to call us patients) sat on the ground and drank tea that he served out of Japanese ceramic cups.

Our emotional intimacy is one of the diamonds of my life. We both had the same strain of existential loneliness and a lust for the Divine. We finished each other's sentences and prayers. We talked about Carlos Castañeda and cars, Bodhisattva vows and good shoes. So obviously, I was a bit in love with him.

Michael was notorious for blurting out disconnected one-liners—poems, koans, personal updates. You really had to try to keep up with his transmissions and multiple personalities.

I don't remember what crisis I was yammering about when Michael shifted from staring out the window to looking squarely at me and interrupted, "She's dying."

It's not protocol to announce to your patient mid-share that your spouse is dying. But we were us, and it made sense. We held our gaze for a long time.

I broke the silence. "Sa Ta Na Ma," I said softly.

Michael said it back, nodding in agreement, "Sa Ta Na Ma."

Sa Ta Na Ma is a mantra loosely translated to: *Birth. Life. Death. Rebirth.*

Over the years, it had become our shorthand for: *Life can be f*cked, but it's beautiful, so let's keep going.*

Sa Ta Na Ma was our way of blessing & releasing. Inhaling the pain as an act of devotion to what we love.

A few years later, Michael told me that he was dying. He passed over 33 days from his cancer diagnosis. I made him playlists for the pain, and I chanted for him daily. He told me that it helped.

Our final text exchange: Sa Ta Na Ma.

*Life can be f*cked, but it's beautiful, so let's keep going.*

My Bless & Release Journal

Re: My baby's birthday. A friend in need.

> *It's my son's birthday! I light a candle for my morning practice, and I bring his total and utterly awesome energy into my heart center. I bless him up and down, and inside out. I pour on every possible high vibration n' virtue. Joy, Resilience, Wisdom, Creativity, Divine Love. It's easy and effortless, and I could do it all day. Happy Birthday, Harper! Mama's got you in the inner world and the outer world.*
>
> *While I'm in the Centering zone, I decide to bless a friend who's exhausted. She's caring for her beloved in palliative care. When we last texted, she said, "Please pray that I can get some rest and sleep through the night, it makes all the difference in this." So, I bring her into my heart center. I speak her full name. I imagine her sleeping deeply when she can. I stream the light spectrum onto the restful vision. I give thanks.*

Chapter 17

Desire higher

I WANT TO MANIFEST...

New love. Being more present to the daily magic and miracles. Resources and peace. Wealth abundance mindset. Being inside the knowing more than I am now. Love. Liberated light work that ignites women, impacts generations, and makes multi-millions. Financial security. Peace and tranquillity. Love. Lucrative career. True freedom. Acceptance and freedom. Inner peace. abundance. The village that holds us all. Expanding my havingness to an automatic state of being. Inner peace. Acceptance. Self-love and self-compassion. Joy, purpose, and belonging. Wealth. Space in my head. Ease. Phenomenal wealth. My life partner. Love in all its manifestations and presence. More trees! Peace and beauty. Financial ease. The ability to trust, be brave, and find love. Confidence. Acceptance that stress is also part of our nature. Peace. That I am totally in control of how I experience this world, and I love myself completely. Freedom. A bestselling book. abundance and impact. A sold-out event that leads to amazing Love and Joy for all. abundance. Peace. Authentic flow. New patterns of connection, care, and flow. Ease.

I've surveyed thousands of people about what they want to let go of. And thousands more about what they want to manifest. The results give me hope in humanity because it turns out that what we truly desire isn't **stuff and status**, it's **states and qualities.** We aren't prioritizing materialism—alleluia!

We want **spiritual outcomes and nervous-system results.**

Our letting-go lists reveal where we're stuck or struggling; our manifestation lists show what we're evolving towards. We want success without sacrificing peace. Heart centred accomplishment.

The 4 Qualities We Most Want to Manifest

1. **Peace.** Ease. Acceptance. Confidence. Freedom.

2. **Joy.** Happiness. Beauty. Deep purpose.

3. **Love.** Self-love. Compassion. Belonging. Connection. Partnership. Community.

4. **Abundance.** Wealth. Financial security. Impact. Resources. Creative flow.

We want energy before outcomes.

This shifts the focus of manifestation from "what I want to get" to "what becomes possible when my energy field is quieted and receptive."

We need inner attunement before outer attainment.

> *Is it possible to be desireless? No. Actually, it is not possible.*
> *As long as the mind is there, its duty is to desire.*
> *[...] the secret is that any desire without any personal*
> *or selfish motive will never bind you.*
> —Sri Swami Satchidananda

According to some Buddhist principles, the highest spiritual intention is to exist in a state of desirelessness. The aim is to be so unified with the Infinite that we want for nothing, unfolding only with the perpetual now. When you realize that the universe exists within you, like, what's more to want?

But to desire desirelessness... well, you can see the irony. Desire is part of the full human experience. I've had this conversation with Buddhist lamas, rabbis, and Unity ministers, and everyone agrees that the spiritual path includes wanting. But... what we want, how we hold that longing, and how we act on our desires define our life.

Heart centered desires consider the potential benefit (or harm) our success may bring to others.

The growth path, which we've established includes desire, is about learning how to hear the Soul's cues and having the courage to act on those directions. When we don't (which happens often), it can push us off track for a season or a lifetime. But these experiences teach us how to stay on track longer—in alignment with the Soul. That's life: we learn through contrast.

Not getting what we want isn't proof that we're not deserving of it. The absence of what we want is not a confirmation that we're wanting the wrong things.

Dreaming stirs up doubts. With blessing, we bring visions and desires into the heart chakra for energizing. AND we work with the heavier energies that surface around those visions and desires. Bless the dream, bless the doubts.

Every time you do the Centering Practice, it's like increasing your wi-fi signal for intuition and flashes of insight. That's how you more clearly hear what your Soul wants for you. Intentionally working with the energy of fear and attraction attunes you to Higher Guidance.

We can't be desireless, but we can have higher desires.

What you run from will chase you

> *If your mind carries a heavy burden of the past, you will experience more of the same.*
> *The past perpetuates itself through lack of presence.*
> —Eckhart Tolle, *The Power of Now: A Guide to Spiritual Enlightenment*

The art and science of manifesting can get really distorted in the personal development space. **Ambition at all costs blinds us to our true motivations.** If you're not aware of what's driving you, you could be in for some sharp detours. Chasing unconscious desires usually involves a big wake-up call.

A lot of our desires—and therefore, aversions—come from the unconscious and subconscious selves.

Metaphysically speaking, every desire conceals an aversion.

I like being really social... I don't like being alone because when I'm alone, I start to fear that I might be alone for the rest of my life.

I prefer silence... Music irritates me because my nervous system is fried, and I know that I need to change a lot about my life in order to heal.

I want to generate 6 figures because I don't want the pain of being rejected by my parents if I need their help.

Desire and aversion are two sides of a coin. They are *both* a form of wanting. I want this. I *don't* want that.

When we're strongly averse to something, the Lower Mind unconsciously creates a desire to run from the aversion. The stronger the desire or aversion, the more intensely we'll get triggered from not getting what we want. Force attracts counterforce. Desperate desire or intense repulsion makes us brittle. And very bother-able.

Instead of confronting and embracing the fear that's our underlying motivation, we believe that manifesting our desire will relieve our problems. But the real problem is that we are in denial that we are running from something.

If "energy can't be destroyed," it certainly can't be outrun. We may as well fess up and bless it. Ultimately, we might decide to change our aspirations or keep them; either way, we will manifest them with less fear and more flexibility.

Blessing our fears, one by one, trigger by trigger, softens our attachments to our desires *and* our aversions. Healthy detachment is a form of courage—which is very magnetic to positive outcomes.

Want to know the best part of figuring out what's been driving you unconsciously? Hands down, it's that you free up massive amounts of energy to manifest your conscious, truly-good-for-you-and-others, beautiful desires!

When you know *why* you want what you want—and that *why* is rooted in Joy and self-honouring—the coast is clear, babe.

Lovin' on my fear

I've had a history of respiratory challenges. Wet winters in Vancouver didn't help matters. One winter, I was so scared of another bout of bronchitis that I made a plan to head to Mexico. I literally said to my friends, "I'm fleeing the city for a few months. Gotta escape to heal my lungs."

Maybe "flee and escape" weren't the best vibes. I manifested a tragic comedy of mouldy hotels and 24-7 noise. I'd walk into a room, my eyes would start burning from the mould, and I'd tell the bellhop not to bother with my bags. This happened at 3 places.

Then I checked into a pretentious concept hotel, but it didn't have window blinds so I was up at dawn. I was getting desperate for sleep, warmth, and fresh air, so I went to a remote jungle house for some silence. It was so cold that I had to wear all my clothes to bed. I wrapped my sarong around my head to keep my ears warm.

Then I resolved to find a cheap cabana and sleep on the beach all day. It was a beautiful morning as I flip-flopped out to the lounger. The sound of ocean waves caressed my frayed nervous system. I took the supine 'n sun position. A happy beach bunny, I started to doze. And then... *ooontz ooontz ooontz...* house music from the loudspeaker hidden in the coconut tree.

I was so exhausted at this point that I started to cry. And oh my God, there was another speaker in the opposite tree, and they fired up some Shakira. I was caught in a Berlin disco-style Latina battle of the bands.

I put my straw hat over my face and sobbed. It was the convulsing kind of crying. The music was so loud no one could hear me.

I was tired of chasing safety. Tired of *running from being afraid* of getting sick again... a fear I had carried for years, everywhere I travelled. Clearly, I could run. But I could not hide.

It was time for some centering. Right hand on my heart. Deep breath. I brought to mind how much I love the ocean, my profound gratitude for Mama Earth, and the sun! *God, I love the sun.*

Then I brought my fear of getting sick into my heart. The heavy worry, the anger, the sadness of all the things I've missed out on because I was congested and coughing.

I poured the light colours all over it. Shimmering, healing frequencies. And I just let my fear relax—on a lounger in my heart. I was in full Acceptance of my situation. I calmed down. I stopped resisting the *oontz oontz* house music and let it move through me.

Then I realized that despite weeks of mould, fatigue, temperature swings, and air conditioning set on "arctic," I actually hadn't fallen sick. What would have given me a lung infection in the past hadn't affected me at all. The fear was in my head. I was fine. I was more than fine. I was lying on the beach in Mexico with Shakira.

At that moment, I decided to change my story. I stopped saying, "I have sensitive lungs." I started saying, "I used to have respiratory issues." Then I stopped talking about it altogether. *I stopped fearing that my fear was going to manifest what I feared.*

When we embrace what we're running from, we get to put it down.

How the lower mind and higher mind manifest

Manifesting is a technology that anyone can learn to work. Crush your goals. Exceed them. Amaze yourself. When you get there, be well. Be full of good energy.

We know people who have used the laws of manifesting—see it, believe it, repeat it—to manifest outward success, but they felt empty when they got it. Out of fear, they jump to the next goal to crush.

The Lower Mind grasps for its goal. That grip just increases the fear and aversion of not getting what's desired. Manifesting from the Lower Mind is like, "What can I get for myself ASAP?" That's a recipe for self-abandonment, greed, exploitation, and a lot of hard lessons.

Desire rides on freewill. You're allowed to want whatever you want, materially, financially, spiritually, sexually, inwardly, outwardly, long term, immediately... But it's only when we start to work intentionally with the heart that we hone in on what we truly desire. Ideally, *what's meant for us.*

Then a shift takes place: from total willfulness to surrender. And that's when concepts like "unity," and "life purpose," and "Joy" really start to come alive within us.

Heart centered visions are nourishing and interdependent. We see others benefiting from our success. This happens naturally when you're using The Centering Practice for manifesting. You'll be visualizing your phat bank account and see yourself wiring some surprise money to your sister. You visualize your ribbon-cutting ceremony, and everyone you love is there with you, soaking up the happiness. You set the goal to buy some acreage, and the visual in your blessing includes the animals and elements of the land. Your energy field lights up with Generosity.

This is really important: reaching ego-centered goals is only temporarily satisfying. I've had this conversation with pro athletes and celebrities who tell me, "I won, and I felt empty." A sign that there was a lot of chasing and proving, and not enough deep connection to their inner life.

The hungry ghost is never satiated. When we nail our ego goals, it immediately asks, *What's next?*

In contrast, when you achieve a Soul goal, you will actually pause to celebrate and integrate it. You will revel in and cherish what you created—and all the people and forces that came together to make it happen. This is key: heart-centered achievements build on each other.

The ego wants fireworks and big punctuations. The Higher Mind likes to weave with Light.

Inner attunement, then outer attainment. What you've created will then show you what to create next. This is how we build Wisdom and avoid do-overs. It may not be easier than the prove-hustle-grind path, but when you arrive, you feel like more of yourself.

Chapter 18

Acceptance changes everything

Acceptance looks like a passive state,
but in reality it brings something entirely new into this world.
That piece, that subtle energy vibration, is consciousness.
—Eckhart Tolle, *A New Earth*

Creating a more ideal future is directly related to truly accepting your present. Acceptance has the texture of Compassion, so it helps you relax and keep creative energy circulating. Acceptance reveals a lot of what's been going on—without gross judgment—and helps you see the best next step.

Manifest-it-quick strategies can gloss over the Acceptance phase. Mostly because we want out of pain ASAP. Makes sense. But fear and pain heal faster when you hold them closer.

I had a friend who was in a heap of debt. She owed back taxes and family loans, and her credit cards were maxed out. So stressful. Of course she wanted to manifest some abundance. Frantically.

Shame had her in a headlock so she couldn't look at the bills or calculate what she owed. It got so insufferable that she wisely got herself in a debtors' support program and made herself an Excel sheet.

A lot of us have been at a similar crucible moment, whether it's related to our business, our bodies, substances, or relationships (which we sometimes use like substances). We find ourselves in a mess, and we seek a methodology to help us mop it up. Smart! Even smarter when it comes with wise counsel and a community cheering us on.

Except that a methodology on its own doesn't guarantee that we tap into true Acceptance. If the process is devoid of self-compassion, we won't move beyond the old behaviour. We have to pair the manifestation and recovery systems with heart intelligence. It's Love, not fear, that keeps us on the wagon.

A blessing protocol—Acceptance—is the energy management that guides behaviour.

My friend had taken the first steps: she had documented her debt and made a plan to chip away at it. But two things were holding her back. First, she was in such a state of self-loathing that doing what needed to be done felt like a punishment. The Excel sheet was more of a sh*t list than a freedom plan.

Second, she was fixated on getting out of debt. And why shouldn't she be fixated on that? Wasn't that the point? No. The point was that debt had to stop being the main character in her story. She needed to no longer identify as someone in debt. It was time for a wealth mindset to take the lead.

That would happen eventually. But only after the Excel doc got buried under negative self-talk and more spending and avoidance. Finally, my friend, like so many of us, had no choice but to resort to radical Acceptance. I think her words were, "F*ck it, I just gotta love myself and do this."

And she did. She blessed her mess and stopped hating herself for getting into it. It became a portal to self-respect and freedom.

Affirmations—but better

I'm in debt, and I accept and love myself.

I'm struggling with wine and weed, and I accept and love myself.

I'm angry, jealous, still grieving, feeling lost, and I did the thing that I said I wouldn't do. And... I accept and love myself.

The affirmation "I accept and love myself" is a powerful methodology when we vitalize the words with our chi—breath, life, Light.

Pain inspires major life reprioritization.

And then, it occurs to us to just love ourselves after all.

Acceptance is a creative force

When you accept a situation as is, you're not signalling to the universe that you don't want change. To the contrary! You're telling it that you can accommodate whatever change is necessary.

You can see what the moment requires of you.

There's suffering. I acknowledge it. And I can also make choices that will end the suffering.

Acceptance is the decision to grow instead of staying stuck. We can't make clear choices if we don't see the truth. If we want to change reality, first we have to get real.

Acceptance is not about condoning bad behaviour. It's not a permission slip for lack of responsibility. It's not feeble surrender, or giving up on the vision, or a lack of faith.

It's by accepting what's going on and not resisting it that things begin to shift. We can even accept our resistance! How is this cosmic kung fu possible? Because Acceptance operates on the frequency of Divine Love. And anything that receives Divine Love grows into a higher expression.

**Acceptance is not a spiritual bypass.
It's devotion to the deeper meaning of life.**

It's one of the fundamental virtues, alongside Resilience, Generosity, Forgiveness—these aren't emotions, they're states of Higher Consciousness.

Stop sending your struggles *eff you!* energy. Force attracts counterforce. When we try to repress our hurt or deny that we have a vice, then the hurt and the vice get more powerful.

Radical Acceptance kicks off deep transformation. What do we mean by radical? No blame. No shame. No complain.

Accepting everything—the welcomed and the unwelcomed—causes us to expand and to heal.

When you're in Acceptance mode, you have more mental clarity to see the next best step. The less energy you waste on resisting what is, the more energy you'll have to command your life. Allow the power to be all yours!

My Bless & Release Journal

Re: The hurtful thing that impacted the relationship.

> *I'm chopping vegetables while thinking about a hurtful, slightly shocking comment made to me by someone I adore. I'm replaying that conversation that took place on my sofa, and I'm hovering above it, watching my past self have the internal reaction of sadness and disgust.*
>
> *Then I see my current self making dinner. I become aware that I'm hurting myself again with this memory replay. I'm reactivating the pain, not healing it. It's creating acrimony and resentment.*
>
> *I'm pressing on a wound that wants to heal.*

Centering time. I breathe into my heart. I think about swimming in the ocean in July in Vancouver. Bliss. Then I become aware that my heart is flooded with golden light. I see the hurtful comment moment happening in the center of my heart. I breathe. I flood my heart with the stained-glass colours of light. Luminous.

The "scene" soaks up the colours. I breathe. I resist the urge to think it through and to rationalize the behaviours. I breathe in the scene, which is intermingling with the dappled light.

I need to be mindful to only focus on that one conversation and not drag in the whole relationship dynamic and dozens of interactions.

This was a very painful event that was connected to the demise of the relationship, so I don't expect the pain to evaporate immediately. But I do feel that working with it on the energy level is the dose of medicine I need.

I take one more concentrated breath; I let the scene rest in the colours in my heart.

I breathe. I re-direct my thoughts to something immediately positive: how grateful I am that I'm going for a walk with a friend after dinner.

After this, I can stop ruminating on it for the rest of the night—this is progress. Over time, the memory of that moment crosses my mind less and less, and with less charge and pain. I feel much more compassion towards us both. It's all okay. It's all meant to be. Even that moment that changed the course of things. If that memory circles back, I breathe into it and let it find some peace in my heart.

Chapter 19

Identification creation

Re-examine all you have been told in school or church or in any book, and dismiss whatever insults your own soul; and your very flesh shall be a great poem...
—Walt Whitman, *Leaves of Grass*

Every transformation has a before + after story

You do not need to improve your negotiation skills so that you can negotiate your worth in the world.

You don't need a checklist of faults that you want to "let go of."

Forget about who in your life needs to change so that you can have more peace or prosperity.

Babe, we know better. We're not playing that game.

We need to build a stronger bridge to our Higher Self so that when our small self is afraid or confused, we know where to turn.

Our greatest creations emerge from our True Identity. And by that I mean *our Divinity.*

> *Nothing is more important to us than our conception of ourselves... especially is true of our concept of the deep, dimensionally greater one within us...*
> —Neville Goddard, *Out of This World*

Successful "before + after" stories have a middle chapter—the part where we let go of identities that don't match our ideal life.

Warning, Dad joke incoming... *What happens when you play country music backwards? You get your job back, your wife back, and your dog comes home.*

Letting go can feel like going backwards. But then it starts to feel like good momentum.

Over the last few years, my life has looked like a big yard sale. I sold my awesome house with an art studio. Now I rent a small apartment by the beach. I got rid of my car. Now I walk. I gave away half of my wardrobe and more than half of my furniture. I abruptly said goodbye to a bad romance and a heap of expired desires. And why stop there? I burned down my decade-long business structure and rebuilt my team—and my ambition.

But let me back up. In and amongst all that radical simplifying, I had to examine my neurotic self-helping, my fear of a punitive God, and the wrath of New Age karma. I was forced (strong word, but big letting go can feel like that) to question every long-held belief I had about true happiness and my identity in the world.

My Soul—with the help of my hormones—sent me some anxiety and panic attacks. This was all new to me. I had no reference point for anxiety or waking up with suicidal ideation.

My days were filled with psychotherapy and energy work. I lay on the living room floor, breathing into my heart, while watching my personality crumble. When my kid went to his dad's for a few days, I'd ferry to a Catholic retreat center and lie on the forest floor, begging the moon for mercy. I am not being poetic. Lying on the mossy rocks in the woods, I would plead for my emotional pain to be absorbed by the Light.

I learned to be gentle where I used to apply force. I accepted that I had a distrust in God's best wishes for me. And when I loved that distrustful part of myself, it freed up a lot of trust.

Success at the cost of my peace became obviously ludicrous. And peace, for the first time in my life, started to look really sexy.

I reoriented my life around my heart. I learned how to bless & release my suffering. And I found out that my Joy was always there. And it will be when suffering visits again. Knowing that keeps me sane.

Letting go of all of the externalities was like having a yard sale of my past accomplishments. It just naturally happened. Now it takes a lot less to make me happy, which is Joy.

Correct indentification

> *The Tao is infinite, eternal. Why is it eternal? It was never born; thus it can never die. Why is it infinite? It has no desires for itself; thus it is present for all beings.*
> *The Master stays behind; that is why she is ahead. She is detached from all things; that is why she is one with them. Because she has let go of herself, she is perfectly fulfilled.*
> —Laozi, *Tao Te Ching*

We tend to lead with our labels: Extrovert. Introvert. Outgoing, easy-going, solo. Super mom. Good guy. Agnostic. Bombastic. Nomadic. Attached. Avoidant. ADD. PTSD. HSP. INFJ. Mani Gen. Gen X. Enneagram 4. Forward thinking. Strong-willed. Soft spoken. Rational. Emotional. Never gives up. A lover. And a fighter.

To manifest your most aligned desires, you've got to let go of some excess identifications.

The Buddha taught that all suffering comes from identification. Which is to say, being overly attached to our image can create difficulties.

Identities are very layered stories that we spend years writing. And then... scene change! Curveball. Life gets very life-y. And you're not someone's honey anymore. You lost it all in the fire. Your body says, "Drop everything and fight for me." That executive position, gonzo. The cash flow dried up. You were in the lead, but dude, now you're cancelled.

If you're a transcendent being, fully aware that you are an emissary of Light traversing through the universe en route to the great void of the Divine, then having your worldly identity stripped from you will be no big deal. Amazing. Send us a postcard from the 5D.

But most of us have invested massive energy in building identity and success. We have life plans (maybe bequeathed to us by family and ancestors). We have amassed obligations… So identity disruption can be very, very disruptive. It's designed to be that way.

Loss ruptures our self-image. We can let go willingly or cling to it. Either way, we're going to be humbled and tenderized. It can be so hard to surrender what's made us feel worthy and powerful.

But when your Higher Self decides it's time to get better acquainted, it lights your life script on fire. The masks burn, and there we are: re-made and re-prioritized.

Ego shedding is how we become truly resilient and radiant.

And by radiant, I don't mean in a shiny, perpetually positive New Age way. I mean, *illuminated.*

The dark night always reveals your Light.

How radiance happens

Some people think that light work is about connecting with your spirit guides and increasing your intuition. And it can be. But it's also about connecting with the most terrified, arrogant, exhausting, and exhausted parts of ourselves. Light work is shadow work.

The hardest part of facing our shadow self is how hard we try not to face our shadow self. Repressed, oppressed, hidden, disgraced. Manipulative, uptight, neurotic. *Eeshk.* Who wants to hang out with that?

But we have to.

At first, our healing is mostly about us: our needs, our boundaries, our desires. This self-centered phase of healing is natural and almost unavoidable.

But eventually that strategy breaks down. Our old identity no longer works. Our habitual patterns and conditioning fall apart. And we realize that healing ourselves is no longer just about us.

At the end of every tunnel that leads to transformation is group Love. For example, if you've been initiated through depression, loss, or overcoming addictions, you may feel called to do what you can to help spare someone else the pain you endured. You want to find others who are suffering, help them, and include them. You become a kind of angel to someone else.

Shadow work is not about being inundated by the darkness. It's about making the unconscious conscious, realizing our Oneness with everyone and everything.

The ego gets cracked open to make space for the Light to emanate. Or we could say that the Lower Mind gets tractor-beamed up into the Higher Mind.

When the ego self experiences a crisis—a loss of a dream, humiliation, an identity in question—its self-centeredness begins to loosen, which allows our True Nature, our Inner Light, to shine through. We finally see how out of alignment with our heart we've been. This is fantastic! Where there was once a lot of fear, there's now a lot more wisdom.

The pain becomes a purification.

> *Barn's burnt down—now I can see the moon.*
> —Mizuta Masahide

In the meltdown, we start to sense a natural yet supernatural force with us. God's hand, destiny, the Divine Mother. Friends standing by us.

This is the really amazing part. The old story that *we're separate and disconnected* begins to fall away.

- Ask yourself, *What identity am I holding on to?*
- The victim or the solution?
- Fear or love?

The wound or the healer?

> **Our heart centered desires come forward.** We reorient ourselves from "me" to "we" thinking.
>
> We become more loving.
>
> Our thoughts, words, and actions become more compassionate. This is what it means to be aligned. *Radiant.*

Let's review

There's correct identification and incorrect identification.

Incorrect identification: *I am my titles and my roles. I am my body. My feelings are "me." I am a reflection of my past. My worth is equal to my productivity.*

No, babe. We're going to bless & release those misidentifications and all the suffering that comes from them. This is a hopeful and joyful process.

Breathe into your heart.

Correct identification: *I am an emissary of Light, and I'm here to werk it.*

What's meant for us is seeking us.

We don't need to be strategic; we just need to be available.

And make space for it to show up.

Chapter 20

Wanting what's meant for you

We've covered the physics of letting go—you've got to transform it. And we've got the science to prove that just *thinking* about light makes us feel better. Soon, we'll look at the framework of Faith.

But before we do that, here's some advice that supersedes the physics and most of what's taught in manifestation culture:

Want what's meant for you.

Does that bring some relief? Or is this an unsettling concept? Probably both.

Just try it. Want what's meant for you. Not someone else's definition of success. Not a grandiose, exaggerated version of fulfillment because we've been told that dreaming bigger is better.

We don't need to contort ourselves into something we're not. We don't need to plead with the deities to have our desires met.

Manifestation motivators and religions have been trying to sell us permission slips to reach our own destinies.

What if the *real* secret is simply to want what's meant for you?

Especially and only for you. Custom designed. Something you can unwrap, then say, *Thank you.*

Through our blessing work, we raise our frequency. And this is how we become very magnetic to what's meant for us.

Text the cosmos:

> You: "*Hi. I'm ready for the life you've been waiting to give me—one that's better than I could have imagined.*"
>
> The Cosmos: *Even if it looks different than your vision board?*
>
> You: "BRB."

Wanting what's meant for us can feel dichotomous. What about the injustice in the world? What about the unfair playing field? What's fair and considerate to desire?

And given the number of identity deaths we go through in one lifetime, how do we know what's meant for us if we're always evolving?

Well, there is one singular desire that every wisdom school encourages: the desire to know thyself. To awaken to your True Identity—which is Love.

Ultimately, we're here to become more loving. That's what's meant for all of us.

It's a long game. And long games are a hard sell in quick-fix societies. Of course, we want to be out of pain ASAP. But we keep coming back to Earth school to learn to love our way through every conceivable high and low.

Let's brake for karma

> *You will live in excuses and victimhood until you understand that freedom is taking full responsibility for your own life.*
> —Reverend Michael Bernard Beckwith

When talking about desire, we have to bring karma into the conversation. Karma is another concept that's been twisted up in self-help and religious ideology. Guilt trips are big business for some religions—and comfortable terrain for the Lower Mind.

Ancient hermetic philosophy teaches that "God neither punishes, nor protects, nor rewards." If you grew up in organized religion or reading New Age primers, this concept is mind-blowing.

Most major religions—and many neuroses—revolve around the belief that a higher power outside of ourselves is keeping score and flagging penalties for our good and bad behaviour.

Yogi and guru Paramahansa Yogananda dismisses that. "Man should blame no one but himself for his troubles. God doesn't reward or punish anyone. Suffering is caused by the misuse of one's own freewill. God has given us the power to cast Him away or to accept Him. God doesn't want us to suffer, but He will not interfere when we choose actions that lead to misery."

Again... does that bring some relief? Or is it unsettling? Probably both.

Buddhism also affirms self-agency. It doesn't see a God-like figure as holding the scales of right or wrong. Instead, it posits that karma—cause and effect—is in our hands.

Karma is training in conscious creation. Karma is not a punishment system from an angry deity.

Your Soul says to you, "Hey, love... did it feel good to act that way?" And you think, "Nah, that was a sh*tty move on my part." Then karma says, "How about you back up and clean it up?" Karma is not a problem; it's a portal.

When we clean up our messes, we find out how powerful we are. Bringing order to chaos brings us closer to our Divine Nature.

Every time you bless your saboteurs, your karma gets lighter. Reframe confrontation into connection... lighter. Flip a grudge into forgiving... lighter. Give your focused positive intention when you'd rather rant... lighter. Give without expectation... lighter.

Blessing disrupts and changes behaviour patterns and tendencies, creating new responses. Blessings break vicious cycles.

Imagine your toroidal field (the donut-shaped bio-magnetic field of the human heart) filling up with light. Brighter. Fuller. Bigger. You're literally outgrowing your karma. This happens through choice. The Soul dispenses lessons, and it's up to us how we meet them: as problems or portals, resentments or assignments.

The Soul is always moving us towards expansion.

Do we preach about karma to victims of unspeakable things? To those in barely bearable hardship? No. No, we don't. The immediate response to anyone suffering is pure, unmitigated, ever-flowing compassion. Always.

Yogananda's renegade take on karma is: "Refuse to be bound by karma; it is an old superstition of the ignorant to believe you cannot change your destiny." Translation: we all have things to clean up, and we get it done with conscious creation.

Karma teaches us the universal law of balance. Everything has to be brought into harmony because that is our natural state—we are returning everything to Love. Karma is the way home.

I have filed my complaints with God. *Are you kidding me with this lesson?* Chronic pain, loss, existential loneliness—they all had me begging for mercy at times in my life. My learning was always the same: Accept it. Not as a punishment but as an assignment. As a multiplier of Resilience and Joy. After Acceptance comes very clear guidance.

When I blessed my pain, I found my power.

> *To every thing there is a season, and a time for every purpose under the heaven.*
> —Ecclesiastes 3:1, King James Bible

Sweet surrender

"Wanting what's meant for you" is not a very sexy advertising campaign. There's no marketing hook about our deficiencies. You don't have to lose weight to want what's meant for you. You don't have to make more money faster to want what's meant for you. You don't need anyone's approval to want what's meant for you.

Wanting what's meant for you is a wise way to surrender. It puts you on the path to deep, deep understanding about how your life works.

This is not a flaky New Age approach to life. It takes a heap of courage and dedication. It doesn't mean you should be passive, or you shouldn't have strong preferences, or that effort doesn't matter. It doesn't mean that you have to give up on your dreams.

Wise surrender is about surrendering to your life right now, dropping in and being present. You pull your attention away from the past and out of the future. Then, from the potency of the present moment, you release older energies that are blocking your dreams.

Wanting what's meant for you is about receptivity, not passivity. There's nothing lazy or naive about it.

"Going with the flow" is active and responsive. You have to be alert to what's happening and choose to move. It's like Eckhart Tolle says, "Life is the dancer and you are the dance."

Wanting what's meant for you is one part trust fall, one part mental ninja move. Relaxed, but laser-focused. Heart breathing and mind-steeling.

You need willpower to attune to the Higher Mind.

Appreciation, contentment, and Faith ground you in your reality.

Wanting what's meant for you is a very graceful way to live.

You accept and work with what *actually materializes* in your life.

You see that missed opportunities mean the right conditions haven't arrived yet. And you can create the best conditions. You don't obsess with "what could have been"—because that denies the power of the Divine. You trust in divine timing.

People, get ready

We need to prepare ourselves to receive what's meant for us. It's always en route, and it's often right in front of us. But if we're not ready for it, we risk having to circle back, clean up, and start again... like lottery winners who blow it all because they lack the identity and internal structure to match the frequency of abundance.

If our energy field is full of opposing vibrations, like lack-thinking, resentment, or fear, then what's meant for us can't penetrate our reality. We have to become a match for it. And how do we do that, my sweet, gluten-free donuts of light?

We let go—we integrate. We forgive! We bless the lack-thinking, resentment, and fear so that it lightens. We use all our tools—the blessing protocols, and meditations, and tree hugging, and salty baths, and kindness and gratitude—to purify our energy field... to ready ourselves for what's meant for us.

Gratitude is the power tool of manifesting.

Like attracts like. Similar thoughtforms attract more of the same. Understanding this will change your whole life.

One doubt magnetizes more doubt until we have a cluster of doubt. One grateful thought evokes more grateful thoughts until we have a beautiful cluster of Gratitude—which is highly magnetic, attracting more experiences to be grateful for. Gratitude is money in the manifestation bank.

We might have to pray to know what's meant for us.

I take my desires to my higher counsel and ask, "Is this a good idea? I mean, I'd obviously love for this to happen..."

And I wait for my answer.

I did this recently on a summer solstice. I spent a week or so really thinking through a fresh life vision. I ended up with a beautiful but, um, *rather bold* future scenario. I was open to a reality check. Maybe I'd need to back away from the vision to keep my health and my life humming along. Because, as I said, peace has become a very sexy proposition to me.

I sat under a willow tree in Stanley Park, Vancouver, and asked for Higher Guidance on the vision board in my heart. I was a bit trepidatious because I knew I had to be willing to drop it. Maybe it was too big, too demanding, too... not meant for me.

I took a deep breath into my heart center and asked, *Should I go for it?*

I didn't get a flash of insight or a counter vision of more glory. My Soul didn't say, *It shall be so, dear one!*

Instead, I heard this very clear response: *Why not?!*

It was lovely and inviting.

And I answered back, *I mean right?! There's no reason why not! Let's do it.*

I think that was the most important part of that ceremony. The "Let's do it" part. Let *us* do it.

Because I know when my Soul drops an idea into my mind, it's not all on me to make it happen; she will follow up with directions. What's meant for me is on my path. I just need to lighten my load and keep walking in the direction I'm meant to go.

I hugged the willow tree, walked home, and wrote out my vision in my very best handwriting. And I placed it on my altar. Every day, I bring that vision into my heart and bless it. All the colours, lighting up my life with the virtues of abundance and Joy.

And whenever doubts surface, I bless them too.

. . .

If I told you that your big dream was *for sure* coming true in the next 12 months, you'd clear the clutter and get a glow up. In other words, you'd get psychologically and spiritually prepared.

You'd be excited, focused, and grateful all at once. *You'd start falling in love with what was coming your way.*

Fall in love with what's coming your way.

I adore the tradition of the great Sufi poets like Rumi and Hafiz, who approached God as the beloved, and us as lovers. This is such sublime devotion. We're in a committed relationship with the principle of manifestation!

Conscious creation creates a beautiful tension of polarities. Receptivity and effort. Spiritual and mental. Trust and intention.

Are you willing to trust the universe as it co-creates with you? Focused positive intention, blessing, is the pin on your map. It anchors you when things get shaky and uncertain.

When we're scared, we still have our intention as a reference point.

A blessed vision helps us tap into the deeper reality beyond goals, strategies, and day-to-day thinking. We learn to direct our thoughts towards the highest outcome, not just as a personal wish, but as a practice of co-creation with the Divine.

5 Ways to Prepare For What's Meant For You

1. Forgive

Resentment and anger are lead weights in your energy field. Bless in all directions. Bless your pain. Bless yourself for struggling to forgive. Bless the people you are trying to forgive. And let it go; appreciate the growth. Forgiveness cleans your energy field like nothing else—allowing you to receive more... and more deeply. When we forgive, we open to the flow of Life Force and what the universe has in store for us—what's rightfully ours.

2. Petition your higher self

Ask, *What would Love do? Is this meant for me?* Asking your Higher Self for guidance is an act of courage. Obeying your Higher Self is grace.

3. Find the others

Seek out the ones who are ahead of you on the path and hear what they have to say. Teachers and sages help raise our frequency and make quantum leaps.

4. Focus on being fuller, not necessarily "bigger"

More full of Love, Generosity, and Joy. This is embodiment, not performance.

5. Continually examine your practices

Ask, *Is everything I'm doing to be well actually helping me to be well? Does this render me more loving?*

Chapter 21

Manifesting alignment

When you do understand, reality depends on you.
When you don't understand, you depend on reality.
When reality depends on you, that which isn't real becomes real.
—Bodhidharma, *The Zen Teaching of Bodhidharma*

Manifestation isn't magic. It's the science of cause and effect.

Go for what you want. Do the inner work and bring it into the physical reality. Find out how powerful you are. Create more, manage less.

Put more energy into creating your ideal reality. And put less energy into trying to control a set of less-than-ideal situations.

Inner work is mostly about cleaning up our energy... creating the right conditions for growth and attraction. Without cleaning out the weeds in our mind (fear, etc.), manifestation may still be possible, but it's much harder.

When we bless to let go, to heal, we're creating more inner space to seed our desires. Then we bless those desires and our manifestations.

The essentials for conscious creation

1. **Have regular identity check-ins with yourself.**

   Are you identifying as blessed or behind? If the alignment is off, there will be trouble. If you perceive yourself as a conscious creator, as Light, then you will magnetize what's meant for you.

2. **Acknowledge your fears—and bless them.**

   Identify the fears and beliefs that bring you down and keep you playing small.

   We tend to resist going into this unconscious territory. It can be scary. Bringing up our denied desires, suppressed thoughts, resentments... this is active engagement with our pain points. It's hard work. It can seem easier to press forward, but that creates more suffering in the long run.

   You know what to do. Consciously interact with your fears. Bring them into your heart center and work with light frequencies. One at a time, over time, clear your fears with purification practices. Write and burn. Process them with yoga, nature, breathwork. Talk them through (and then stop talking about them).

   This makes a fertile ecosystem in your mind, where you can plant your well-thought-out desires, aspirations, and dreams.

3. **Love what you have—it's the fuel for abundance in all forms.**

   When we're constantly yearning for things to be different, our Life Force dips.

Being content is under-appreciated. Contentment leads to inner harmony. Inner harmony makes way for Gratitude. And Gratitude is the foundation for abundance.

Perpetual wanting, needing, desiring—it's tiring just thinking about it. When you relax into your contentment, the mind cools down. When you let what you have be enough for today, you're healing.

Being happy with what you've got is where all good things come from.

4. **Become a vibrational match for what you desire—that starts with letting go.**

Praying for things to be different isn't always the most effective way to get what you want. Why? Well, if you're praying *not* to be broke or alone, what are you focusing on? Being broke and alone.

We want peace, but we're asking from our anger.

We want to be wanted, but we're not accepting others.

We want it to be easier, but we're always overworking.

You can see the incongruency.

We hear a lot about becoming a vibrational match for what we want, being the person we want to fall in love with, seeing ourselves as wealthy. Those identity and visualization techniques can be very powerful, however...

The subconscious mind must be congruent with higher desires. Success only grows in the right conditions. No goal is achievable if the environment is toxified with fears and complaints. We must clear the weeds, so they don't choke the seeds.

Becoming magnetic to our desires is a two-pronged approach: cleanse AND visualize. As we heal, we manifest more of what we truly desire. We can reprogram our unconscious and subconscious mind through devotional practices—with focused positive intention.

5. **Think nourishing thoughts—they're magnetic.**

   Energy follows thought.

   You think it, you begin to feel it.
   You feel it, you begin to believe it.
   You believe it, you begin to see it.

   Our thoughts become our chemistry.

   Choose nourishing, life-affirming thoughts—thoughts aligned with the virtues of Love, Compassion, Inclusiveness, Joy, and Generosity.

   Then FOCUS on those thoughts.

6. **Build the connection to your Higher Self—every day.**

   All the practices for awakening are really about becoming more intimate with your Soul until you realize that there is no separation between your daily life and your Divinity.

7. **Include others in your success plans.**

   What you wish for your own health and happiness, wrap that wish around all beings.

8. **Focus on what you want to expand.**

   Our degree of focus directly correlates to our creative power. Depending on what we're focusing on, we're creating more peace or chaos—inner and outer.

   We can select the thoughts we want to amplify. Remember, if you don't want to think about something in particular, *think about something else.*

   Concentration is penetration. When we concentrate on a thoughtform, we're pressing it into our energy field so that it can flourish.

   When we're in a truly focused state, the mind rests. We're in the flow, and the thinking quiets down. Then the Higher Mind can drop in.

9. **Take the time to get clear on what you want.** Conscious creation is like weaving with strands of Light—one strand at a time creates a sturdy tapestry. Every image is being projected on the future you're stepping into.

   See and feel your desire clearly before you start energizing it. When you're ready, colour in the details.

10. **Word it well.**

    Words carry energy and speak your pure intention. Frame your intentions and desires as a positive affirmation. Begin your sentences with gratitude. *Thank you for... I'm so grateful that...*

    Use the present tense. *I am creating... I am connecting... I am inspiring...*

    Include all beings and all kingdoms of nature as recipients of your fulfillment. *May all be so blessed.*

11. **Work with light.**

    Light is Life Force. Our bodies need it, our brains love it, our Souls are made of it. When you use light as a tool for healing or creating, you're working with the most powerful substance in the universe.

12. **Work with the elements.**

    We're made of the Earth's elements. Earth, water, fire, air, ether. When you're visualizing your success, incorporate elements into what you see. Like the quality of the sun, the sounds of nature, being by the water.

    When we call the elements into our visions, we're creating inner balance. When we practice blessing protocols while outside, in nature, we get energetic support from the Earth's magnetic field. It's like a vitamin cocktail for the thoughtforms in our energy field.

13. **Detach from the outcome—offer it up.**

    As Hindu theology teaches, "Act fully, release the results."

    Obsessing about our desires actually messes with manifestation. Obsession is a form of clinging, which slows energy circulation.

    Hold desires and thoughts loosely. Then the desire and thoughtforms can extend beyond your energy field and gather more energy and momentum to manifest your dreams. We bless & release our visions so that they can fly into the cosmos and return to us—fulfilled.

14. **Ritualize to formalize.**

    Rituals amplify intentions. Light a candle, say a prayer, chant a mantra. Set up an altar. Do the vision board. Throw a party and make a declaration. Make vows. Rituals make the mundane sacred and reinforce your gaze on the goal.

15. **Act with faith.**

    And if you don't have faith, take action anyway; the faith will come.

    Faith is a deep teaching in letting go. It's the foundation upon which all manifestation sits.

    Faith is trusting that the Light is there even when it's dark—and you're that Light!

Faith is like the railroad track you lay down in the substratum—beneath the material world. And our vision is the train. Without faith, our visions cannot reach their destinations and become reality.

And because we can trust we'll be supported by the Divine *whether or not our vision becomes real*, our aspirations are free to move forward and pick up momentum.

Faith—not force—carries our visions forward.

When doubt or impatience creeps in, don't try to override it. Bring it into your heart and let it unwind. Thank your doubt for reminding you to strengthen your faith—that's the very purpose of doubt.

Doubt isn't the opposite of faith: impatience is. Impatience is focused on surviving. Impatience can't see the bigger picture because it's too busy panicking right now.

Doubt and impatience aren't personal failures. They're shadow fragments reminding us to choose higher-quality perspectives. Faith is one of the highest points of view we can have.

One way to develop the virtue of Faith is to pay very close attention to the fact that Life has always come through for you. This isn't blind faith; it's proof of concept.

You're still here, wanting to love and be loved, being breathed into by Life itself.

What happens if you're low on Faith? You can ask for more. Just turn to the Divine with willingness and ask for it, "Help me find my Faith." Leave the door open a crack, and the Divine will come in and support you.

Faith isn't something we "have" or need to hold on to. We embody it. We're transmitters for the higher energy that is Faith. We clear our inner space to become more Faith-full.

Faith feels like peaceful excitement. It's the deep conviction that by blessing beliefs that no longer serve us and blessing beliefs that do, our highest good will come to us. We will be rewarded for our dedication.

Faith alone isn't enough to manifest a vision. You have to meet it with action. The "work" involved in making something real is the work of merging inner devotion with outer action.

Faith magnetizes and attracts elements and circumstances into your energetic electromagnetic field to manifest dreams and visions into reality.

Faith is one of the most direct routes to the Higher Mind. It grants us access to divine direction—which always leads us back to Joy.

Q+A with V.S.

V.S. is a metaphysical practitioner I've been collaborating with for 10 years. Her wisdom is woven through this work. Here's a direct Q+A with her...

When is the ideal time (day/lunar time/season) to start manifesting?

Sunday, Thursday, and Friday are great days to begin a cycle of manifestation. Sundays are ruled by the Sun—the ideal day of the week for devotional practice. Thursdays are ruled by Jupiter—the energy of expansion. Fridays are governed by Venus—which is all about Divine Love and Higher Consciousness.

It's best to do your practice at the same time every day for a month or more. Rhythmic sequences are more powerful than haphazard investments of time. The spring and fall equinoxes and summer and winter solstices are also great times to start a cycle. Or anytime your heart desires!

How often should I do The Centering Practice?

As often as you'd like. The emphasis is on repeating it cyclically, daily, weekly, or bi-weekly. Another point is to do it at the same time every time—invest in that space.

Can you manifest for other people?

Teamwork is dreamwork! When the other person is actively engaging in cleansing and purifying their auras through specific Yogic and meditation practices, and learning to become conscious of their mind and thoughtforms, then yes, it is possible to support them deeply through their manifestation process.

How far into the future can I manifest? Is this even a consideration?

You can manifest in this particular lifetime for this incarnational cycle. A lot of good karma has to be generated in order for the manifestation to concretize in our physical reality. You cannot rush this process because past karma stands at your doorway until it's neutralized with accuracy, diligence, and devotion.

Does The Centering Practice create good karma?

Yes, whenever you are working with the heart space and offering up something, you gain positive karma. You are reverberating at a more refined frequency, your heart chakra is glowing, and you are experiencing forgiveness and are cleansing and purifying the elements of your aura. Your heart-mind is expanding, and your view has become very vast. This is all very beneficial and generates great positive karma.

What is the key to conscious manifestation?

Aligning your thoughts, words, and actions. Also, a very big key is to have an extra-large heart chakra through giving, through practicing generosity, through embodying the virtues, and through living a heart centered life.

What blocks abundance/manifesting?

Living in the past, holding onto past resentments, bitterness, ruminating in old spaces, disconnection from gratitude and graciousness, self-worth tumbleweeds, obsession and possession about how the manifestation will work out—these stand in the way of bringing our vision into this physical dimension.

Did I manifest this pain, suffering, heartache? How? Why?

Your entire life and all your life experiences are your own creation. You are manifesting your reality all of the time. However, it's best to note that what you are manifesting is *unconscious* in nature. Hence, many experiences may seem hostile, stifling, painful, and depressing. When the energy bodies are not cleansed and purified, that which gets projected onto the fabric of life may be of a grosser, denser nature, causing us to experience pain, suffering, and heartache. So we bring it into the heart center to refine and clarify our minds and our aura. This diligent devotion to purification and refinement leads to peace, abundance, and Joy.

What's the balance between not having expectations, which can result in disappointment, and also caring strongly about the things I'm trying to manifest?

You can definitely have expectations, why not? At the same time, know fully that you cannot rush anything. The more contracted your mind, and the less your receptivity, the more time and space it takes to bring the elements in towards your final goal. When your thoughts, speech, and behaviour *align*, and your frequency is vibing at a higher, more refined pace, your dreams will unfold before you. Obsessing about the final result will energetically create a barrier to your dreams. Stay grounded and live in the present.

Chapter 22

The Centering Practice for your life

Every human is endowed with the power of blessing.
Blessing starts in wishing good, in willing good for others.
People must continuously exercise their power of blessing.
Through blessing much goodwill comes to earth.
—Torkom Saraydarian, *The Power of Blessing*

Centering reminders

For those of us who tend to **lead with our heads...**
you get to relax with this practice.
No thinky think. All flow.
You're in your heart center now.
For those of us who lead with **gut instincts...**
you can go slow for a minute.
You're in your heart center now.
For the **feelers going with the flow...** you can let the light do the cleansing work.
You're in your heart center now.

Centering doesn't just have to be for negative feelings or something you're trying to repair. You can use it just to send extra love and happiness—to your kids, your beloved, all of your people. You can heart center and bless projects, first days of school or work, birthdays, any celebration!

Your shame? Center it.

Your fear of the future? Center it.

Your shame about feeling ashamed? Center it.

The constant striving that is wearing you down. Pangs of fear when you think about getting what you desire. Bring it all into your heart center.

And your desires? Heart center them!

The details of your visions, scene by scene. Center them.

The enthusiasm, faith, light, love. Work from your heart center!

The certainty and determination that's required. Centered!

The Centering Practice

Bring it into your heart. Heal and manifest.

1. **Breathe.** Place your right hand on your heart for a few breaths.
2. **Positive thought.** Bring to mind a beautiful memory, feeling, or virtue. This helps your mind relax.
3. **Gold light.** Imagine warm, golden light filling your heart.
4. **Bring what you're healing or manifesting into your heart.** See the scene, moment, word, symbol, or thought in the center of your heart.
5. **Light spectrum.** Shine rainbow colours on what you're blessing—like light moving through stained glass. Work with colours that feel soft but dynamic and alive. These are healing frequencies.
   Pinks, peach tones, golds, minty greens, sky blues, light purples.
6. **Add in virtues if you like.** You can project or speak higher qualities into your heart center, such as Compassion, Love, Joy, Forgiveness...
7. **Important: Let what you've blessed relax in your heart.** There's no need to fixate on it or analyze it. Now that you've done the energy work, let the expansion happen.

Repeat as you like, in daily moments or as a long-form meditation.

The Centering Meditation

- **Purpose.** The Centering Practice can be completed as a meditation in this longer form. The process stays the same, but with the extra time the experience becomes deeper.
- **Duration.** Practice for 10 to 20 minutes. Linger at the end with a few steady breaths.
- **Timing.** You can do this any time of day, multiple times a day if you like. Mornings and before sleep are ideal.
- **Posture.** Anything goes—seated in lotus, lying down, or walking. Eyes open, gazing at a candle or fixed point, or eyes closed. If you're practicing this in stillness, ideally face east—to be aligned with the rising sun.
- **Breathing**. Breathe at a natural pace through your nose.
- **Guidance**. Allow for more time and space in each of the steps for the colour frequencies and to create sensations to deepen the experience.
- **Gold light**. Imagine the quality of the golden light. Feel it warming your heart. This golden light is filling and preparing your heart space.
- **Bring it into your heart center.** What does the scene look like? What's the moment? Who's there with you? Where are you? If you are using a word or symbol, imagine it forming letter by letter, curve by curve, over your heart.
- **Light spectrum**. Imagine the colours shining through stained glass. Alive, dynamic, and moving over your heart. Imagine them one at a time.
- **Virtues**. Speak the higher qualities

Centering Boosters

Manifesting with the centering practice

One at a time. We create thoughtforms and visions in our inner world to be manifested in our outer world. When you're doing The Centering Practice to manifest, work with one vision at a time. So, rather than imagining your ideal life, visualize one aspect of it—focus on a vision of wellness, or prosperity, or a relationship. You could work with visions for specific parts of the planet or your community. Bless each vision one at a time.

See success. Visualize the fulfillment of your desire—a completion scenario. If you want to win a gold medal, see yourself on the podium, not doing the training.

Include the Earth elements. Earth, water, fire, air, ether... how are they represented in your vision? Are you outside, and the sun is shining? Are there water fountains, candles burning, stars in the sky, flowers everywhere, sweet air? Feel the elements.

Include others in your success. A Centered vision is a celebration of our Divine Nature—it uplifts everyone involved. How do you see others benefiting or feeling the positive effects of your fulfillment? Are they in your vision or somehow connected to it? When we plan to use our fulfillment to also benefit others, we increase our success. The universe supports goodwill because it's the natural order of things.

Refine it. Take the time to refine your vignettes so they're what you really want. Once you start visualizing regularly, you don't want to change it up too much. Play it on repeat.

Give thanks when you complete The Centering Practice—for the realization of that vision! Then, repeat the process for your other visions.

Release it. Release all of your visions into the sky until they fully disappear from your sight.

Let Faith handle it. No need to obsess or tug at it. Focus on being centered, and Creation will take care of the rest.

Stay with it. Bringing a thoughtform to life isn't a one-time visualization practice; it's a long-term commitment to a spiritual practice that bears fruit in divine timing.

Energizing with virtues

Virtues are Soul qualities, principles of Higher Consciousness. They are very, very healing energies. You could think of virtues as the offspring of Divine Love—the mama. If we imagine Divine Love as a brilliant sun, then all the rays emanating from her are unique virtues.

When you're centering and working with the colour frequencies in your heart, you can also bring in some virtues. Just speak the word "Love" or "Forgiveness" into your heart. Or see the word "Gratitude," or feel the energy of Joy. Project higher qualities into your heart center. Raise the vibration!

Virtues...

- **DIVINE LOVE** is the ultimate inclusiveness. Unconditional. Spacious. Honouring. Divine Love neutralizes polarization. It's unity consciousness.

- **COMPASSION** is the wish for all beings, no matter their actions, to be free of suffering and the causes of suffering. Compassion dissolves judgment and division into Love and interconnectedness.
- **WISDOM** comes from the Soul, not the intellect. Wisdom sees how everything and everyone is connected. It always leads to the Universal Mind.
- **FORGIVING** is the heart's natural inclination. The Soul will always guide you to forgive. Forgiveness is an energy reset that brings us back to our True Nature—Love.
- **RESILIENCE** is our ability to respond from the heart's intelligence. It's not about armouring up—it's about adaptability and meeting everything with Love. We bend so we don't break.
- **RADIANCE** is our suffering alchemized into Light. The ego relaxes, and Soul Light pours into us. Then we begin to reflect that Light!
- **JOY** is the experience of pure Life Force moving through us. It's always there, foundational, eternal, spacious. We often get to Joy by clearing up limiting beliefs and misidentifications—tapping into our True Nature.
- **ACCEPTANCE** is the ultimate openness. Instead of denial or rejection—which are such draining distractions—all things are brought into the heart center.
- **LOVING KINDNESS** is unconditional friendliness. We use our freewill to choose Love...benevolence. Loving Kindness meets the situation without criticism or cynicism.
- **FAITH** is believing that the Light exists even when it's dark—and you are that Light! Faith is required for conscious creation and shifts to occur. It's a state of surrender to Higher Guidance.

- **GRATITUDE** is the most direct route to presence and inner strength. It's a solvent for low-frequency emotions. Gratitude is one of the most universally mentioned practices in ancient spiritual teachings. It's a generative, creative force.
- **GENEROSITY** is the capacity to realize our interconnectedness. It opens us up to the evolutionary force of Life. Generosity is nobility of spirit, our capacity to be in the flow of life.

Hand gestures

If a healing topic you're blessing is particularly sensitive and heavy, **use hand gestures** to "scoop" the discomfort into your heart. The physical motion will help settle the mind.

Write a love note

- **For healing:** If your emotional suffering is feeling very difficult, write a love note to your suffering—pencil to paper—and hold it to your heart as you work with the light frequencies and breathing.
- **For manifesting:** You could write out a description of your fulfilled vision and hold it to your heart. Energize, energize!

21 Days

Work on a particular healing topic or manifesting a vision for **21 days in a row** or as long as you like. Really give 'er... but hold it lightly.

Same time

Consider doing The Centering Practice at the **same time every day.** A reliable rhythm is nourishing for your nervous system and cues your spiritual guides that you are ready to work.

Morning centering

Set a loving intention for the day. Right hand on the heart. Breathe in your intention or your virtue, and pour on the colours.

Evening centering

Bring the day's highlights and lowlights into your heart. Let it all rest so that you can rest.

Singing, chanting, omming

Self-generated sound helps the vagus nerve relax. And sound acts as a vibrational healer. When sound and rhythmic movement work in conjunction with the breath, emotions stabilize. And with more balanced emotions, we're able to tune into higher frequencies from our throat chakra and resonate there for as long as our heart desires. Singing out loud and humming softly are very healing. Singing mentally or quietly so there's no sound is actually incredibly powerful—you're working in the inner worlds.

Mantras

Playing, speaking, or chanting mantras during a Centering Practice is like pouring vitamins on whatever you're working to heal or create.

Nature

Any time we practice outdoors, we're exchanging prana, Life Force, with all of the elements—earth, water, fire, air, ether. First, always give gratitude to Mother Earth, and then open yourself to soak up the element's energy on what you're healing or manifesting.

The Centering Practice for relationships

We can do centering for:

1. **two-way dynamics** within a relationship.

2. for our **personal patterns** in relationships.

3. for the **history** of a particular relationship.

4. for a relationship that we have or want to **move on from**.

    - **Bless one dynamic at a time.** If you need to bring healing to a relationship, this is key: only work on one particular relationship dynamic at a time. Don't try to cover the entire history of the relationship. For instance, bring in an image of a moment in a conversation, or focus on one word or emotion that is causing disruption. We heal in layers.

    - **Choose your people.** You can focus on one person or a group, present or past.

- **See them in their highest form.** You could do a Centering Practice where you bring the other person into your heart, and you see them at their highest good. You visualize them being joyful, generous, whole. *You're seeing them in their fullest, most beautiful, and most powerful form.*
- **See *both of you* in your highest forms.** You could do a practice where you bring *both of you* into your heart in your highest forms.
- **Forgive.** Work with your breath and the colour frequencies. Bring the relationship into your heart. You could simply ask the question: *What does the energy of Forgiveness feel like?*
- **Seek resolution.** You could bring them into your heart center and repeat the words, "Divine resolution."
- **Commit.** Where there is more perceived tension in a relationship, it's good to give it more time and energy. You could do a longer meditation focused on a relationship (about 11 minutes is very effective). You could also commit to doing this daily for 21 days.
- **Optional send off.** It might be satisfying and effective at the end of a bless & release practice to see the relationship in a container, a sphere of rainbow-coloured light, and release it up, up, up to the sky. Let the container float as high as you can imagine until it's a small pinpoint that dissolves in the atmosphere.
- **End with gratitude.** Always end with thanking your Higher Guidance and the other person.

The Centering Practice for your body

- Your body hears everything your mind says. Bless your body and it becomes your ally. **Remember the basis of health is energy flow.** You're the healer. And you're working with energy, light, breath, and focused positive attention to bring Life Force where it's needed. You're giving the congested emotion in the body exactly what it needs to move on: Love.
- **Choose only one facet of your physical situation to bless & release**. It could be the emotion around your physical challenge, the place in your body where it comes to visit. Or your relationship with your body itself. It could be a diagnosis. It could be a memory or a word that symbolizes what needs to heal.
- If you feel called to, **place your hands** where you'd like to bring healing to your body.
- You could see yourself scooping the pain from part of your body and **bringing it into your heart chakra** for rest and balancing.
- What often happens when we do The Centering Practice for our bodies is that an internal dialogue begins with what we're trying to heal. Stay curious and gentle with the physical condition. Be compassionate and understanding with your feelings about it. We need to be really steady here. Yes, we want to be free of illness as soon as possible. This practice is about blessing what's happening in our body to neutralize emotions and raise our vibration.

The Centering Practice for mother earth and the world

Everything we have, everything we are, is because of Mother Earth. Our bodies are made of her elements. Our buildings are made of her body. As are our vehicles, technologies, and cures. Every relationship we have... is her. We are from and of her. We owe Mother Earth EVERYTHING.

With so much happening on the planet, we can sometimes feel helpless. We want to go beyond donations and spiritual platitudes. Doing The Centering Practice on behalf of Gaia is a way to have a more conscious relationship with our planet. This is for communion and homage. The intention deepens our restoration.

- Use The Centering Practice to focus on parts of the Earth that need healing. Places that you want to manifest more balance, protection, nourishment. See the locations, the trees, the neighbourhoods in your heart center and do the blessing work.
- Consider adding the virtue of Gratitude into your practice. Praise Mother Earth for pulsing through you and all sentient beings.
- Bring one specific emotion or aspect of your pain about the state of the world into your heart. Work gently in layers. This is a form of service for the collective. Thank you.

Chapter 23

You're a Super Blesser

14 Signs That You're A Super Blesser

1. **The old dramas cease to be as interesting.** You used to jump on an issue and debate it out. But now you think... *to each their own*. You make decisions based on what will bring ease and connection.

2. **You become less triggerable**. Instead of reacting, you respond. You feel more spacious, resilient, and loving, so you can hold your feelings and other people's opinions with more grace. When you think about the best way to respond to a situation, you consider what's best for everyone involved. (By the way, this is also the essence of great leadership.)

3. **Fixing other people is not your primary concern.** Of course, you want to help others, but your ego's need to be the saviour isn't running the show. You realize that everybody's healing path is their own, and you can support them without interfering. This is liberating for everyone.

4. **Loving all parts of yourself is genuinely energizing.** You meet the most difficult aspects of yourself compassionately. You have respect for your strength. And with that *depth of Love*, you know that you can accomplish *a lot.*

5. **Mutual dignity is always your intention.** Respecting others is as important to you as respecting yourself.

6. **You get curious and lean into the pain points.** Babe, you're here for it all. You're genuinely curious about what's happening underneath the surface and what would bring about the most healing. Emotional intimacy is your favourite.

7. **You reframe every challenge that comes your way by asking: *How big of a problem do I want to make this?***

8. **You *gently* silence your inner critic.** You don't put down the part of you that's putting you down. You're the parent. You lovingly reassure your inner critic that you've got it handled.

9. **Loving people is your superpower.** You're stoked to be your most loving self, no matter what. You walk away from hard moments thinking, *Well, I got to be loving in that situation.* It affirms your aliveness!

10. **Contact with your Soul is your top priority.** You do the work to tune into and follow your Higher Guidance. Devotion to your Inner Light is your spiritual fitness.

11. **You see everything as an opportunity to become more loving.** Absolutely everything. You recognize that suffering is not a punishment, but a guide to your Truth.

12. **Your self-reliance is unshakeable.** You know that you're capable of powerful healing and creation. This self-awareness deepens your connection with the Divine and everyone you come into contact with.

13. **You don't chase. You choose.** You hold your clear desires lightly—and that's magnetic.

14. **You want what's meant for you.**

Centering

Center everything in your heart. Balance with a few breaths. Apply compassion. Bless it with the light. Release it back into your energy field. It works every time.

Your point of view begins to expand. You start seeing the beauty in everything—and pointing it out to others.

When you offer grace to yourself and others, older versions of you fade away. Don't contract around them. Let them loosen up and become something new.

Let the light have its way with you.
Honour your Divinity.
Transform.

You're going to have a mature and loving relationship with your shadow self. Your Inner Child will stop acting up and derailing your plans. Self-compassion will become your anchor in the storm.

You will genuinely reshape your thoughts, words, and actions. The incoming higher frequencies will bring every kind of abundance into your life.

I hope that I run into you, and you tell me that you've become "someone who's great at letting go!" And what you'll mean by "letting go" is that you *let things in.*

Instead of pushing away your feelings or trying to make them behave, you do something radical: You bring them into the center of your heart. Gently. Continuously. Blessing them.

You've become your own healer—the spiritually mature adult of your life, an alchemist who turns incorrect thinking into Truth; someone who's freed up their energy to really give and receive Love.

What a beautiful life. This is what's meant for you.

Thank you

Thousands of people helped shape *Bless & Release.*

Every lovely human who has ever been in our Centered Membership gave me reason to think and serve more deeply. You kept me accountable to the Light. To everyone with a Centered Planner who tells us what you love and what we could make better... thank you! To everyone who DMs me some Love after doing The Centering Practice... bless you.

For everyone who answered the *Letting Go & What Do You Want to Manifest? Survey...* and everyone who answered my questions on Instagram at all hours... and everyone who shouted back answers to me at speaking gigs... thank you! You gave me so many seedlings.

Thanks to the most generous focus group a writer could ask for: Teresa Barney, Inesa Baski, Karen Beal, Christina Bjorndal, Bobbi Billman, Heather Brandon, Shelly Day, Aranzasu De La O, Tara Disch, Heather Ferreira, Melanie Frome, Jenny Goldman, Marie Gough, Kim Guthrie, Deb Hann, Tatjana LaPointe, Karen Larkin, Ren Lis, Amy Lynn, Gina Madonna, Corri Megan, Barbara Merrithew, Sara Marie Eley, Sarah Skahan, Nicole Moody, Danielle Nelson, Jane Needham, Miriam Ortiz y Pinño, Paula Parker, Michelle Ramseth, Glory Ramsey, Charity Rogers, Kimberly Salinas, Nance Scott, Skye Shelton, Amira Sookram, Jennifer Szesula, Vanessa Sullivan, Kate Swoboda, Chez Tansey, Erica Wheeler, Carina Yeap.

This book is a full-on co-creation. To V.S., my noble and most gifted metaphysical practitioner-sister, thank you for infusing absolutely everything with high mindedness and Light. Beyond the beyond.

Team D dug into every word and theory until we got it right. *Fifteen drafts worth of loving care! A delivery and launch campaign of stellar proportions!* And they made it beautiful in every way. To these smart hearts, I bow: **Shyanne Batchelor, David Di Pardo, Mellissa Last, Lea McGing, Jenn Orajay, Dana Tartal.**

And we did this all while building the Centering app. Holy. Moly.

Deeply blessed, deeply grateful.

About

DANIELLE LAPORTE's spiritual direction has reached over 40 million people. She's the Founder and CEO of Centering—the first app of its kind for spiritual wellness.

Her podcast, WITH LOVE, DANIELLE, is in the top 0.5% of shows. She's a member of Oprah's Super Soul 100.

Her books include *Bless & Release, How to Be Loving, White Hot Truth, The Desire Map,* and *The Fire Starter Sessions*, alongside her popular Centered Planner system. Her Centered Membership and Leadership Curriculum have supported facilitators in 30+ countries.

Danielle was Executive Director of a futurist think tank in Washington, D.C. Now she speaks about the intelligence of Love.

She lives in Vancouver, B.C. You can find her most places @daniellelaporte.

V.S. is a metaphysical practitioner who has worked closely with Danielle for over a decade to create meditations and practices and provide astrological and energetic guidance. Originally from India, she draws from multiple wisdom traditions.

Your Bless & Release bonus resources

There's more where this came from.
Everything you need to go deeper with The Centering Practice is waiting for you—free, and always growing.

Claim your free resources at:
daniellelaporte.com/blessbonus

Inside, you'll find:

- The Centering Practice guide (PDF)
- The Centering Practice and Centering Meditation — extended audio, with original music by Grammy-winner Chris Sholar
- Bonus lists, practices, and extras from the book
- Illustrations, digital wallpapers, and more

We keep adding to it. Check back.

Own the book? Get the audio or ebook.
The audiobook is 5+ hours, narrated by Danielle, with original music by Grammy-winner Chris Sholar. The ebook is yours to search, highlight, and return to. www.daniellelaporte.com/bless

Connect with Danielle

Stay connected with Danielle:

With Love, Danielle—available wherever you listen to podcasts

@daniellelaporte

@daniellelaporte.inc

@daniellelaporte

@daniellelaporteofficial

thedaniellelaporte.substack.com

daniellelaporte.com

Index

www.ingramcontent.com/pod-product-compliance
Lightning Source LLC
Chambersburg PA
CBHW032003050726
47590CB00006B/2033

* 9 7 8 1 7 3 4 6 7 9 4 3 4 *